ALL I CAN MANAGE, MORE THAN I COULD

If people want to have headaches among the overtones, let them. And provide their own aspirin. Hamm as stated, and Clov as stated, together as stated, nec tecum nec sine te, in such a place, and in such a world, that's all I can manage, more than I could.

Samuel Beckett *to* Alan Schneider

ALEC REID

ALL I CAN MANAGE, MORE THAN I COULD: AN APPROACH TO THE PLAYS OF SAMUEL BECKETT

GROVE PRESS, INC.
NEW YORK

First published by The Dolmen Press, Dublin, 1968; revised edition, 1969; first American edition, revised 1971.

Library of Congress Catalog Card Number: 71-139264

ISBN: 0-394-17767-3

Manufactured in the United States of America

Distributed by Random House, Inc., New York

First Printing

To Beatrice, with love

CONTENTS

Part One

Part Two : Beckett's Dramatic Work

ACKNOWLEDGEMENTS

The germ of this essay was sown all unwittingly by Mr. Beckett himself during a conversation, but he cannot be held responsible in any way for its subsequent development; to all my direct questions of fact, he has replied with unfailing patience and courtesy. Four personal friends have in different ways given me essential encouragement, William Webb, George Begley, Tim Harward and John Hurst. Peter Lennon, Charlotte Davis, Nöelle Johnson, Frances McElwaine and Michael Philcox have gone to great trouble to provide photostats and details of productions. To Mr. and Mrs. Ralph Slazenger my thanks are due for generous and constructive hospitality at a crucial moment; finally, I would like to express my gratitude to Liam Miller of the Dolmen Press, without whose patience and support this study would never have been started or completed.

For permission to quote from copyright material the author is indebted to Samuel Beckett and to his publishers: to Faber & Faber and Grove Press Inc. for the quotations from the plays; to Calder & Boyars Ltd. for quotations from *Molloy* and *Proust;* to The National Theatre (London) for George Devine's programme note to his production of *Play;* to Calder & Boyars Ltd. for quotations from Madeleine Renaud, Harold Pinter, Alan Schneider, Jack MacGowran and George Devine, which appeared in *Beckett at Sixty—a Festschrift,* published by them; to *The Village Voice, The Chelsea Review, Columbia University Forum, The New York Times, The Observer, The San Quentin News* and *Time Magazine* for comments on Beckett's work; and to Faber & Faber and Oxford University Press, New York, for a quotation from Louis MacNeice.

Alec Reid

Fiskardo
Powerscourt
Ballybrack

January 10th 1968

PART ONE

Something about Sam

Beckett's plays stay in the bones. They haunt me sleeping and waking, coming upon me when I am least aware. Sometimes a stray bit of conversation heard by accident on a bus or in a restaurant brings home one of Vladimir's and Estragon's "little canters". Sometimes I find myself actually reacting like Clov or like Hamm or, more often, like both simultaneously. Sam's characters seem to me always more alive and more truly lasting than those in the slice-of-life realistic dramas with which our stages to-day abound.

Alan Schneider.

The farther he goes the more good it does me. I don't want philosophies, tracts, dogmas, creeds, way outs, truths, answers, *nothing from the bargain basement.* He is the most courageous, remorseless writer going and the more he grinds my nose in the shit the more I am grateful to him.

Harold Pinter.

I do not know what Beckett thinks of women, but I know that he understands them profoundly from the inside. If his plays manage to affect us and move us (and if they did not succeed in invading our sensibilities they would not be played throughout the entire world), it is because Beckett, in spite of his modesty, manages to express his immense compassion for all human life and because he is one of those exceptional men to whom love and lucidity are on the same level.

Madeleine Renaud.

This book confines itself to the plays of Samuel Beckett, with special emphasis on the impact which they produce on an audience in a theatre. It offers no philosophies or dogmas, no interpretations — only descriptions. I have attempted it because, like countless thousands all over the world, I find my life has been made richer by Beckett's work and I want others to see his plays for themselves, to experience them directly, and perhaps to find in them some of the comfort and excitement which I have done.

Seen from the outside, Beckett's rise to fame is a strange story. A little-known Irish author, who since 1929 has been producing short stories, poems, and novels, suddenly achieves international recognition in 1953 with his first performed play, *En Attendant Godot,* a piece where virtually nothing happens and the title character never appears. While *Godot* provokes the liveliest debate amongst critics, philosophers and literary men as to its very meaning, it also makes an immediate impact on non-specialized audiences, is translated into a score of languages, and is seen by millions of people from Finland to the Argentine. In 1969 comes world recognition with the Nobel Prize.

There is a second, a deeper paradox. Although a brilliant and sensitive craftsman, Beckett has been striving for the last twenty-five years to pare the formal elements in his work down to the bare minimum. Despite his formidable mastery of words and his early, sometimes pedantic, literary elegance, he now seems intent on the destruction of language. One of the most subtle and erudite thinkers alive, he will admit to only four certainties — that he has been born, is living, will die, and, for reasons unknown and unknowable, cannot keep silence. He does not assert that life is hopeless, for that would be a definite statement and he has not the knowledge sufficient to make it. Godot has not come this evening but has promised to come to-morrow. Admittedly, he may have said the same thing yesterday, but next time perhaps he will keep the appointment; who can be sure? As Beckett himself has said, "The key word in my plays is 'perhaps'." Contrasting his own work with Joyce's, he once remarked, "the more Joyce knew the more he could. He's tending toward omniscience and omnipotence as an artist. I'm working with impotence, ignorance."

Here we come to the heart of the matter. Beckett is agonisingly conscious of the human predicament, the universal uncertainty, the universal helplessness, the universal dumbness. He feels driven on to make some attempt to voice the general anguish, but how can this be managed? How can the chronically impotent achieve a statement, or the chronically ignorant know what to say? How can emotions, volatile and fluid by their very nature, be faithfully expressed in static, definite words? How can the inherently irrational and formless be given shape and order and still stay true to itself? We might as well try to carry sulphuric acid in a tin. Whenever he attempts to work with ignorance and impotence, the craftsman in Beckett must reject imposed form since form implies selection and therefore a degree of certainty. For the same reason the poet in him must get beyond the limits of words, and the thinker must move beyond the realm of pure intellect. Beckett's world can have no definable frontier, "no outside", to use his own phrase. Speak he must, even as he knows the impossibility of an achieved statement, but what to say, and how, and to whom?

And what of us who hear or read? How are we to respond? Intellect alone will not provide an adequate answer since Beckett deliberately shuns the normal wavelengths, the consecutive reasoning process. Furthermore, how can we reasonably hope to find certainties in the signals of a man seeking to transmit uncertainty? At the most we can feel corresponding emotions, can experience the same sense of mental weightlessness, of claustrophobia, of bewilderment, of anguish, of compassion; thereby we ourselves become more aware. To borrow a phrase from Louis MacNeice, Beckett's truth "is not of a statement but of a dance", not of the intelligence alone but of the whole sentient being.

So in this study we argue that Beckett's plays must be considered not for their message but for their impact, not for their philosophy but for the feeling they evoke. Because of Beckett's deep humanity, his work is essentially an art of goodwill, creative not destructive. It is difficult to describe, and in one sense it is beyond critical analysis. We can merely suggest an approach to it; the rest the reader must live out for himself.

Before we turn to the plays, we must say something about the author himself. Throughout his life, quietly but uncompromisingly, Beckett has avoided every form of personal publicity. He is naturally reticent, unassertive, with a deep respect for the privacy of others, and a considerable impatience with the spurious, impersonal world of press parties, public relations and the rest. On one of the rare occasions when he has talked to a journalist, he remarked that writers are never interesting, and for himself at least, it is the work that matters. Only one justification, therefore, is possible for any discussion of Beckett the private individual as distinct from Beckett the writer. Over the past fifteen years a legend has grown up about him which leads to a fundamental misconception of his work. Thousands of people — billions as Estragon would say — will unhesitatingly identify him as the author of *Waiting for Godot,* and, although they know nothing else of him or of his writing, they yet have a clear, insistent image of him as a gloomy, arrogant, desiccated egg-head, the dramatist of dustbins, cripples, and cosmic despair, comprehensible, if at all, only to the highest of highbrows. To Beckett personally this would not matter in the least. As he wrote to Alan Schneider, his American director, after the disastrous opening of *Godot* in Miami, "Success and failure on the public level never mattered much to me, in fact I feel much more at home with the latter, having breathed deep of its vivifying air all my writing life up to the last couple of years . . . . For the moment all I can say and all I want to say is that this Miami fiasco does not distress me in the smallest degree, or only in so far as it distresses you." A man who can think, feel, and write like this needs no one to fight his battles for him, but unfortunately the widespread image of Beckett as an inhuman intellectual affects the general appreciation of his work. It frightens people away, and to no purpose. While writing this study I have become increasingly convinced that if more were known about Beckett himself, more people would come to his plays and come with that open approach which the work demands. That is why these personal details have been added.

Those who do not know much about Beckett are usually very surprised to hear that he took an active part in the French Resistance for nearly two years, and that for the next two and a half he was in hiding from the Gestapo. The circumstances under which he came to join the Resistance are highly illuminating. At the end of 1931 Beckett, then a lecturer in French at Trinity College, Dublin, suddenly resigned, left Ireland, and spent the next five years moving about Europe, now in Germany, now in Austria, now in England, finally settling in Paris in 1937. When the Germans invaded Poland in 1939, Beckett happened to be in Ireland spending a month's holiday with his mother. He hurried back to his flat in Montparnasse, but at first he declined to involve himself in a war which, as he insisted, was no concern of a neutral Irishman like himself. Once the Germans occupied Paris in 1940, however, this attitude of detachment did not last long. Beckett soon became incensed at the Nazi treatment of the Jews, among whom he had many close friends. The constant public humiliations — every

Jew was forced to wear a yellow Star of David stitched onto his clothing — and the almost daily shooting of hostages presented a situation in which, as Beckett has said almost apologetically, "I couldn't stand with my arms folded." Anger led to action. By the end of 1940 he had become actively involved with a Resistance group with agents dotted all over France gathering details of enemy troop movements. The information, some of it seemingly very trivial, found its way to Beckett scribbled on bus tickets, old envelopes, cigarette packets, anything, and his job was to collate it, edit it, type as much as possible onto two sheets of paper, and forward them to another agent to be micro-filmed and eventually transmitted to London. Beckett refuses to attach any importance to this work — "boy-scout stuff" he calls it — but in August, 1942, the group was betrayed, and out of eighty members, less than twenty survived. Beckett and his wife Suzanne were alerted and got away barely half an hour before the Gestapo came for them. For the next four months they were, as Sam puts it, "on the trot", making their way through enemy territory, liable at any moment to be recognised or denounced, executed then and there, or sent to almost certain death in the concentration camps. At last they crossed into Unoccupied France ending up at Roussillon, a village high in the mountains behind Avignon. Here they remained in semi-hiding until the German collapse, Beckett working as a farm labourer during the daytime while in the evenings he wrote *Watt*, a strange, fantastical, comic novel set in the country round Foxrock, County Dublin, where he had been brought up. As he has explained, this helped to take his mind off the war and the German Occupation. For these two and a half years Beckett's life and Suzanne's depended literally on his ability to pass himself off as a French peasant, and to earn enough money by the sweat of his brow to pay for their food. As soon as he could move about freely again, he hurried back to Ireland to see his mother, but he was now so thin and so gaunt that many of his old friends failed to recognize him. These are things which we should remember when we hear Beckett described as a remote intellectual in an ivory tower. More than most people he has lived close to death every minute of the day and has seen those around him butchered suddenly and ruthlessly. He has known fear, suffering, hardship, but also that indestructible determination to stay alive and go on, which we find again and again in his work.

People who have formed their picture of Beckett only through the legend are also greatly surprised to hear of his genius for companionship, a remarkable ability to make those coming in contact with him feel the richer for his mere presence. "Sam," said one colleague who worked with him in difficult circumstances just after the war, "is the sort of person you could wander off with and watch rats swimming in the river, and you'd both feel you'd spent a useful afternoon." The word "both" is significant, for Beckett always imparts this sense of something shared, of someone coming along with you. The same friend goes on to describe him at a tea party in Dublin talking to some students, "giving them everything he could, all they wanted; with it, with them, although there was a whole generation between them."

This gift comes from an instinctive recognition of what the other person needs and a remarkable generosity in providing it. In this context Brendan Behan, whom Beckett liked and admired, had a characteristic story. Once, in Paris, Behan found himself under lock and key due to some temporary financial embarrassment. Beckett hearing of it, sought him out, and then, in Brendan's words, "He paid them what I owed them, and he took me away, and he gave me ten thousand francs, and a double brandy, and a lecture on the evils of drinking." A nicer sense of priorities would be hard to imagine.

This sensitivity extends far beyond those with whom Beckett has immediate personal contact. Asked by the American critic, Tom Driver, if his plays deal with those facets of human experience which religion must also deal with, Beckett answered:

> Yes, for they deal with distress. Some people object to this in my writing. At a party an English intellectual—so-called—asked me why I write always about distress. As if it were perverse to do so! He wanted to know if my father had beaten me or my mother had run away from home to give me an unhappy childhood. I told him no, that I had had a very happy childhood. Then he thought me more perverse than ever. I left the party as soon as possible and got into a taxi. On the glass partition between me and the driver were three signs: one asked for help for the blind, another help for orphans, and the third for relief for the war refugees. One does not have to look for distress. It is screaming at you even in the taxis of London.

This compassion, like his courage, is implicit in everything that Beckett has written since the war.

There is something peculiarly ironic in the idea of Beckett as an unfeeling arch-intellectual. He could easily have been a brilliant university teacher, but at twenty-six he threw up a highly promising career, because, as he said, he could no longer bear the absurdity of teaching to others what he did not know himself. He has always had a liking for the anti-academic joke — at Trinity he successfully lectured to the University Modern Languages Society on a non-existent group of French poets called *Les Convergistes* — and no one has exposed the follies of pseudo-intellectualism more hilariously yet more ruthlessly. Consider, for example, the following passage, taken not from the plays, but from one of Beckett's novels, *Molloy*. The hero has been describing how during the winter he wraps himself up in swathes of newspaper under his great-coat:

> The Times Literary Supplement was admirably adapted to this purpose, of a never-failing toughness and impermeability. Even farts made no impression on it. I can't help it, gas escapes from my fundament on the least pretext, it's hard not to mention it now and then, however great my distaste. One day I counted them. Three hundred and fifteen farts in nineteen hours, or an average of over sixteen farts an hour. After all it's not excessive. Four farts every fifteen minutes. It's nothing. Not even one fart every four minutes. It's unbelievable. Damn it, I hardly fart at all, I should never have mentioned it. Extraordinary how mathematics help you to know yourself.

For all its passionate concern with truth, and its unflinching readiness to face facts, this is scarcely the report one would expect from a learned academic; indeed two earnest commentators have gone so far as to describe it as a howl against scientific procedures and pundits. A strong suspicion remains, however, that Beckett thoroughly enjoyed writing it. We must never forget that he is essentially Irish, with all the national irreverence for sacred cows — his own as well as other people's.

Far from being some kind of thinking machine or disembodied intelligence, Beckett possesses, to an unusual degree, that nice co-ordination of physical and mental which the Greeks valued so highly. This is apparent the moment one sees him, a man, in Schneider's phrase, with 'the head of a Physics or Math professor set atop the torso and legs of a quarter-miler'. It comes as no surprise to learn that he won his 'Pink' for cricket at Trinity in the same term that he was elected to a Foundation Scholarship in Modern Languages as the result of a highly competitive examination. Meeting a stranger, Beckett at first is taut and wary, almost like an animal, but presently he relaxes, a process visible in the angle of the head and the way he holds his arms. If he is upset or embarrassed it is equally obvious, the great head slumps forward, the hands, if he is seated, begin to rub together between his knees and then, as one close friend puts it, Sam can become very mulish. His voice similarly reflects his state of tension, ranging from a dry, donnish tone sometimes described as a rasp, to the warmer, reassuring accents of the Dublin professional man with a Trinity College background. For him, movement is as eloquent as speech and in his plays the two are inseparable. Thus he will speak of lines that can only be delivered looking left or looking right, with the head up or the head down. To think of so closely integrated a man or of his work as purely, or even predominantly, intellectual is to see but a fraction of the whole and to misjudge accordingly.

Shy, friendly, modest, lucid, generous, compassionare, these are the words which people who know Beckett and have worked with him use again and again. Thus encouraged, we may approach Beckett's plays with less fear. They will look strange, utterly unlike anything we have seen before, but, provided we can keep ourselves receptive, we may find them moving and positive.

A New Kind of Drama

When we first see a new form of painting or listen to a new kind of music, we realize that we have to make an adjustment in ourselves and our attitude if we are to get the best out of the experience. So it is with the plays of Samuel Beckett.

(Programme note by George Devine to the National Theatre production of *Play*, at the Old Vic, London, April 7th, 1964.)

This study of Beckett's dramatic work seeks to establish two basic premises — that Beckett, as George Devine says, has created a completely new kind of play, and that in so doing he has greatly enlarged the scope of the theatre. It will examine his methods but will not attempt to explain his plays. Its concern is with impact not interpretation, and its aim is to make easier that adjustment in ourselves and our attitude which is necessary before we can get the best out of the experience which Beckett has prepared for us.

The first point to be established is that Beckett has deliberately designed his plays to be performed by actors for an audience sitting in a theatre or beside a radio. He means them to be experienced immediately, as the sounds come at us across the footlights or out of the loudspeaker; they are not intended to be read from the silent, immobile page, and least of all are they, as one scholar has suggested, running commentaries on Beckett's novels. They are pieces of theatre, needing to be performed if they are to make their full impact, as a symphony needs to be played or a ballet to be staged. So Beckett will describe the initial run-through of a text with actors as a "realization" of the play; and when it is performed publicly, he will say that it has been "created".

Beckett did not write his first play until he was over forty, but from the very beginning of his career as a dramatist, he has shown an uncanny instinct for what works in the theatre. He knows just what he wants and can explain it precisely. Jack MacGowran, one of the two outstanding interpreters of Beckett's work in English, thus describes the value of Beckett's co-operation in a production. "His visual sense is so harmonious, that he cannot happily accept second best in acting, design, lighting or direction. In these matters he is extremely specific, as the balance of all the elements that result in the final product is a delicate but positive one." Similarly Clancy Sigal, who watched him at rehearsals in London in 1964, found Beckett eminently practical. "He is crucially interested in the problem of the stage space in which the players manipulate themselves . . . . his interventions are almost always not on the side of subtlety but of simplicity . . . Gently and firmly Beckett guides them (the players) to concrete, simple and exact actions." Beckett is also acutely conscious of how the conditions of presentation will affect his work. *Waiting for Godot,* he feels, does not lend itself to staging in the round — "it needs a very closed box", — while *Endgame* benefits from a small theatre.

Beckett finds that writing a play is quite different from writing a novel. It is easier, more relaxed. This may seem surprising, but the reason is simple enough. When a man writes a piece for performance in a theatre, he at once subjects himself to certain external requirements. He must so construct his play that the actors can be seen and heard, and he must mould it into some framework of acts and scenes. Such limitations are the basic rules of the game, and if they are not observed the piece cannot be performed. With the novel, however, it is quite different; the author has complete liberty. He can abandon a character whenever he likes, he need not even finish a sentence or ever trouble himself about a paragraph. The only limitations are those which he imposes upon himself. Beckett says that when he sets out to write a novel, he is entering a jungle, an area of utter lawlessness where no rules of any sort apply, and that he finds the change to working on a play like coming out of night into light. The dramatist is restricted, but Beckett feels about these limitations much as Wordsworth did about those imposed by the sonnet form; they are at once a curb and a comfort.

It is precisely because he can so clearly distinguish between the novel and the drama, because for him each is a distinct form, that Beckett succeeds in both. As a correspondent in *The Times* put it, "What Mr. Samuel Beckett does is always more surprising than it should be, because it always, if sometimes paradoxically, belongs entirely to whatever medium he has chosen for it." An interesting parallel suggests itself here and an equally interesting contrast. Goldsmith could write an excellent novel, *The Vicar of Wakefield,* and, if anything, an even better play, *She Stoops to Conquer,* each belonging entirely to its medium. In contrast, Joyce's one play, *Exiles,* does not succeed because it is not theatrical. It presents people discussing a situation, not a situation with people living through it.

In Chaucer's time, the highest compliment one could pay a horse was to call him horsly, to say that he was unmistakably a horse, possessing to a high degree the qualities which distinguish horse from all other animals. In the same sense, Beckett's plays deserve to be called theatrical. They cry out to be acted on a stage — a sure sign of authentic drama — and they produce in us an effect peculiar to the theatre, that immediacy of something experienced directly as distinct from the more remote impact of something described. To secure this, Beckett draws on every resource at the disposal of the dramatist, words, movements, costumes, scenery, sound effects, lighting and so on, but he goes on to fuse these into a new, indissoluble entity. He is the chemist mixing oxygen and hydrogen to make water, the composer weaving separate instrumental parts into a symphony. It is not the words, the movements, the sights, severally which produce the impact; it is the new experience evoked through their combination on stage. This process involving eye, ear, intellect, emotion, all at once, we shall call total theatre.

If we are to grasp the process fully we must be at an actual performance; anything less is like trying to appreciate an Impressionist painting from a verbal description or a black and white reproduction. We can get some faint idea of it, however, through a brief extract from *Krapp's Last Tape*. First of all, let us imagine ourselves in a theatre. Then, when we have understood how the passage relates to what has gone before, let us read it aloud, paying faithful attention to the pauses marked in the text.

The stage in front of us is dark except for a pool of strong white light shed by a lamp hanging over a table in the centre. At this table we see Krapp, a shabby old man whom we have already watched fumbling short-sightedly with his keys, and have already heard talking to himself in a cracked but distinctive voice. Now he switches on a tape-recording which he had made on his birthday many years ago. We *hear* Krapp-at-39, "sound as a bell", as the tape claims, and "intellectually at the crest of the wave — or thereabouts;" but at the same time we *see* the old man on the stage, short-sighted, shuffling, coughing, no longer able to remember what the tape was about. In that moment Krapp's words are immaterial; sight and sound combine to make us know in one brief second the flight of thirty years. Time was, time is; to this favour must we all come.

The voice on the tape is describing how Krapp sat by the canal one cold November afternoon, throwing a rubber ball for a small dog as he watched the house where his mother lay dying and waited for the blind in her room to be pulled down for the last time. By playing on our senses Beckett evokes the whole experience for us very vividly; we feel the wind, see the dull, wintry colours, finger the ball, hear the dog yelping. But as we listen, we become aware of something else, of three distinct sound-patterns. Gradually we distinguish an even-paced measure for narrative speech, a slower, long-drawn-out lyrical tempo, and a brisker, harsh, sardonic tone, and we notice the periods of silence marking the change from one rhythm to the next. From the interplay of these rhythms we gradually realize that Krapp-at-39 is torn by two radically opposed elements in his character, and that the conflict still racks the old man sitting at the table in front of us. The sound-patterns do not depend on any "interpretation" imposed by the actor or the director. They are inevitable, deliberately constructed by Beckett through the words he has chosen, the way he has arranged them, and the pauses which he has put down to separate them. We must hear the passage if we are to feel the texture of the whole experience.

TAPE: —bench by the weir from where I could see her window. There I sat, in the biting wind, wishing she were gone. (*Pause.*) Hardly a soul, just a few regulars, nursemaids, infants, old men, dogs, I got to know them quite well — oh by appearance of course I mean! One dark young beauty I recollect particularly, all white and starch, incomparable bosom, with a big black hooded perambulator, most funereal thing. Whenever I looked in her direction she had her eyes on me. And yet when I was bold enough to speak to her — not having been introduced — she threatened to call a policeman. As if I had designs on her virtue! (*Laugh. Pause.*) The face she had! The eyes! Like . . . . (*hesitates*) . . . . chrysolite!

Detail of sensation. Narrative.

Lyrical.
Mood changes.

Quickening to narrative.

Sardonic.

Lyrical.

Attention to colour.

Quickening through narrative to sardonic.

The sound of the laugh marks climax of the sardonic movement. The pause is essential for the change to lyrical. Note how much is achieved from the laugh to the resumption of the narrative — only ten words are used. Krapp recognizes rejected opportunity.

(*Pause.*) Ah well . . . . (*Pause.*)

22

I was there when — KRAPP *switches off, broods, switches on again*) — the blind went down, one of those dirty brown roller affairs, throwing a ball for a little white dog as chance would have it. I happened to look up and there it was. All over and done with, at last. I sat on for a few moments with the ball in my hand and the dog yelping and pawing at me. (*Pause.*) Moments. Her moments, my moments. (*Pause.*) The dog's moments. (*Pause.*) In the end I held it out to him and he took it in his mouth, gently, gently. A small, old, black, hard, solid rubber ball.

(*Pause.*) I shall feel it, in my hand, until my dying day. (*Pause.*) I might have kept it. (*Pause.*) But I gave it to the dog.
Pause.
Ah well . . . .
Pause.
Spiritually a year of profound gloom and indigence until that memorable night in March, at the end of the jetty, in the howling wind, never to be forgotten, when suddenly I saw the whole thing. The vision at last. This I fancy is what I have chiefly to record this evening . . . .

Back to narrative.

Note precision of detail, especially colour making the scene vivid and urgent.

Change to lyrical with the pause.
Note the repetition of 'moments'.
Emotion evoked through sound.
Back to narrative.

Repetition evokes emotion.
Precise detail, hammering the moment home at us.
Back to lyrical.

Krapp recognizes rejected opportunity.
Back to narrative.

Lyrical.

Narrative.

A pool of light on a dark stage, a tape-recorder, an old man listening to a story about a dog and a ball, just under 250 words — what could be simpler? Yet we have watched a human being tear himself to pieces, and we have suffered with him. There is nothing highbrow or abstruse here, no symbols or learned allusions, nothing calling for specialized knowledge of any kind. All we need is to watch and to listen in the same way as we watch and listen to any other play or film, or to the television. Beckett has often said that his plays are very simple; the difficulties are of our making, not his.

As a rule, Beckett's characters use ordinary words and short sentences. They do not indulge in philosophical or moral arguments, they seldom soliloquize and they never preach. Movement as much as speech is one of the essentials of drama, and so Beckett keeps his people busy. Their actions may not be spectacular, but — and this is inherent in the idea of total theatre — every move is part of the overall experience, as eloquent as any words. Here is a fair example of Beckett's dialogue, taken from Act II of *Waiting for Godot*.

On stage are four characters, two friends called Vladimir and Estragon, a blind man Pozzo, whom they have just helped to his feet, and his servant Lucky, still lying on the ground. In Act I, Pozzo, then in full possession of his sight, had talked to Vladimir and Estragon, and had made Lucky do some pathetic tricks, before taking him to a fair to sell him. Now twenty-four hours later, Pozzo is blind and no longer answers to his name though he responds to both Cain and Abel. Vladimir and Estragon, chronically unsure of everything, begin to doubt whether the first meeting has ever taken place. Estragon aims a savage kick at the still recumbent Lucky, stubs his toe, and howls with pain.

POZZO: What's gone wrong now?
VLADIMIR: My friend has hurt himself.
POZZO: And Lucky?
VLADIMIR: So it is he?
POZZO: What?
VLADIMIR: It is Lucky?
POZZO: I don't understand.
VLADIMIR: And you are Pozzo?
POZZO: Certainly I am Pozzo.

Swift, staccato question and answer as Vladimir with increasing excitement, moves towards a certainty or at least a solution of a problem of identity.

VLADIMIR: The same as yesterday?
POZZO: Yesterday?
VLADIMIR: We met yesterday.
(*Silence.*) Do you not remember?

"Yesterday", a reference to Time which Pozzo balks at. Hence the silence which halts Vladimir. When he resumes, it is with the slower, more formal, "Do you not remember?" as distinct from the more urgent, "Don't you remember?"

POZZO: I don't remember having met anyone yesterday. But to-morrow I won't remember having met anyone today. So don't count on me to enlighten you.

Pozzo closes the incident in measured, complete sentences. He moves away from all talk of Time . . .

VLADIMIR: But —
POZZO: Enough. Up pig!

. . . and from the place where such talk could happen.

VLADIMIR: You were bringing him to the fair to sell him. You spoke to us. He danced. He thought. You had your sight.

Vladimir tries desperately to link all four persons, "You", "Him", "Us", into one shared event. Short sentences again to suggest movement.

POZZO: As you please. Let me go! (*Vladimir moves away.*) Up!
Lucky gets up, gathers up his burdens.

Pozzo is off-hand conversation-ally and literally.
Vladimir's move is more than a physical shift.

VLADIMIR: Where do you go from here?

POZZO: On! (*Lucky, laden down, takes his place before Pozzo.*) Whip! (*Lucky puts everything down, looks for whip, finds it, puts it into Pozzo's hand, takes up everything again.*) Rope!

Pozzo has now finished with Vladimir and Estragon. He con-centrates on Lucky and on departure. His words become staccato again.
Lucky's actions, though not pain-ful in themselves, reveal his

relationship to Pozzo and show in visible terms an anguish beyond the physical, something comparable to that of Lear or Oedipus.

Lucky puts everything down, puts end of the rope into Pozzo's hand, takes up everything again.

This action, which unites the couple, is as visible and meaningful as the giving of the ring in a marriage service.

VLADIMIR: What is there in the bag?

Long question form, not "What's in the bag?" Loss of interest or admission of failure by Vladimir. Playing for time.

POZZO: Sand. (*He jerks the rope.*) On!
VLADIMIR: Don't go yet!

Monosyllables. No communication.

POZZO: I'm going.

Action.

VLADIMIR: What do you do when you fall far from help?

Long question form again. Is Vladimir still playing for time?

POZZO: We wait till we can get up. Then we go on. On!

Pozzo replies in long form to Vladimir, i.e. keeping his distance, but uses monosyllables to Lucky for action.

VLADIMIR: Before you go tell him to sing!
POZZO: Who?
VLADIMIR: Lucky.
POZZO: To sing?
VLADIMIR: Yes. Or to think. Or to recite.
POZZO: But he's dumb.
VLADIMIR: Dumb!
POZZO: Dumb! He can't even groan.

Pozzo is surprised here. Hence monosyllables to Vladimir with whom he is again involved. Vladimir equally bewildered also reverts to monosyllables.

26

VLADIMIR: Dumb! Since when?
POZZO: (*suddenly furious.*) Have you not done tormenting me with your accursed time! It's abominable! When! When! One day, is that not enough for you, one day like any other day, one day he went dumb, one day I went blind, one day we'll go deaf, one day we were born, one day we shall die, the same day, the same second, is that not enough for you? (*Calmer.*)
They give birth astride of a grave, the light gleams an instant, then it's night once more. (*He jerks the rope.*) On!

'Since when?' Time again. Salt in Pozzo's wounds. Note structured pyramid of eloquence, each "one day" being a step to the apex. No metaphor.

The anger subsides. Pozzo knows a moment of compassion, so language and rhythm become slower, more solemn.
It is night, once more, literally and visibly. Evening has been falling as they talk. Pozzo's compassion has gone, hence "On!"

Exeunt Pozzo and Lucky. Vladimir follows them to the edge of the stage, looks after them. The noise of falling, reinforced by mimic of Vladimir, announces that they are down again. Silence.

Pozzo and Lucky go spiritually into the dark. The sound of their fall and Vladimir's mime leave us in no doubt that in every sense they are down and out.

Behind the words, independent of them yet emphasizing them, is a progression, an ebb and flow of action reflected in the tempo of the speeches. Something is taking its course but we could never sense it unless we were actually present at what is going on. Considered in isolation, the actions, the ideas, the speeches, the stage "business", the scenery, are all commonplace and unexciting. When these elements are fused together in the theatre, however, when we can experience the totality which Beckett has made from them, we are held spell-bound.

This impact, out of all proportion to its apparent causes, more closely resembles that of music than that of language; Beckett himself has spoken of his work as "a matter of fundamental sounds . . . . made as fully as possible." He uses words not exclusively as vehicles to convey idea, but always for the effect they produce in a theatre during a performance. In his own phrase, they are one form of "dramatic ammunition". So we must never hope to find any sustained argument like the soliloquies in *Hamlet,* the discussion of Nationalism and Protestantism in *Saint Joan,* or the examination of Mr. Worthing's matrimonial credentials in *The Importance of Being Earnest.* Instead Beckett executes elaborate fugues of point and counter-point, strophe and anti-strophe, silence and sound. The comparison with music is inescapable.

ESTRAGON: In the meantime let us try and converse calmly, since we are incapable of keeping silent.
VLADIMIR: You're right, we're inexhaustible.
ESTRAGON: It's so we won't think.
VLADIMIR: We have that excuse.
ESTRAGON: It's so we won't hear.
VLADIMIR: We have our reasons.
ESTRAGON: All the dead voices.
VLADIMIR: They make a noise like wings.
ESTRAGON: Like leaves.
VLADIMIR: Like sand.
ESTRAGON: Like leaves.
   Silence.
VLADIMIR: They all speak together.
ESTRAGON: Each one to itself.
   Silence.
VLADIMIR: Rather they whisper.
ESTRAGON: They rustle.
VLADIMIR: They murmur.
ESTRAGON: They rustle.
   Silence.
VLADIMIR: What do they say?
ESTRAGON: They talk about their lives.
VLADIMIR: To have lived is not enough for them.
ESTRAGON: They have to talk about it.
VLADIMIR: To be dead is not enough for them.
ESTRAGON: It is not sufficient.
   Silence.

VLADIMIR: They make a noise like feathers.
ESTRAGON: Like leaves.
VLADIMIR: Like ashes.
ESTRAGON: Like leaves.
   Long silence.
VLADIMIR: Say something!
ESTRAGON: I'm trying.
   Long silence.
VLADIMIR: (*in anguish*). Say anything at all!
ESTRAGON: What do we do now?
VLADIMIR: Wait for Godot.
ESTRAGON: Ah!
   Silence.

Like music, Beckett's work must be heard to be effective. The voice is as important as an orchestra, the silences are as important as the sounds, and the sounds as important as the meaning. Beckett will speak of leading up to a pause and going away from it as others might of a rhetorical climax or even a physical action. The pauses are always shown on the printed text, of which they form an integral part no less than the words surrounding them. A simple but vivid instance of Beckett's use of words for their sound rather than for idea occurs in the passage from *Krapp's Last Tape*. Consider the repetition of the word "gently". It is hard to see what difference the second "gently" makes to the sense; but we have only to hear the sentence to realize how inevitable it is in terms of sound. It would not be true to say that Beckett uses words regardless of their meaning so that the sensuous impact would register equally well whether we knew English or not. There is no analogy with "scat" singing where the sounds need not be words, or, if they are, will have no logical meaning; the parallel is rather with "blues" singing where the lyric has meaning but where the voice and the music are at least as important to the total impact.

At a play by Beckett we hear words but they are only one part of something bigger, and so our response, which is to the whole experience, is predominantly direct and sensuous, not indirect and analytical. The strength of Beckett's plays lies not in what they say to the world at large, but in what they do to each spectator personally. When, in George Devine's words, we submit ourselves to the experience which Beckett has prepared for us, we are making ourselves vulnerable; we cannot tell what the piece will do to us. This knowledge can come only

29

after the experience, but our responses must and will relate to something already in us. If we respond to the experience at all, we are almost certainly discovering something in ourselves, unrecognized until now, or we are realizing a little more clearly who and what we are. As Maurice Nadeau says, "Le son de sa voix dans nos oreilles, c'est notre propre voix enfin retrouvée". To some people this is highly disturbing, to others deeply reassuring. Whatever the response, it will be strong precisely because it springs from our deepest subjective feelings. We cannot remain impassive. With Beckett it is very much a matter of those who are not for him being violently against him.

The area of experience with which Beckett is dealing is a place where reason does not operate, a province of the emotions not to be entered by intellectual analysis, but by direct, sensuous response. Therefore it is as pointless to look for a logical, universal "message" behind Beckett's work as it is to look for such a message behind a symphony or a sunset. The author is presenting an experience not an argument, truth not statement, and we must respond each in our own terms. Thus C. Bandman, writing in the *San Quentin News* described a performance of *Waiting for Godot* at the California State Penitentiary in the following words. "It was an expression, symbolic in order to avoid all personal error, by an author who expects each member of his audience to draw his own conclusions, make his own errors. It asked nothing in point, it forced no dramatized moral on the viewer, it held out no specific hope." This is the essence of Beckett's theatrical technique. Not only *Godot*, but each of his plays, is an experience from which he expects every member of the audience to draw his own conclusions, make his own errors. As Professor Kenner remarked of *Endgame*, "The play contains whatever ideas we discern inside it; no idea contains the play." So one critic, a devout and sensitive Roman Catholic, calls *Godot* a statement in dramatic terms of the wretchedness of Man without God, while another, equally sensitive but a convinced Existentialist, sees it as "A general expression of the futility of human existence when man pins his hope on a force outside of himself." Both interpretations are equally valid and equally irrelevant since Beckett is not concerned with any religious or philosophical beliefs — "I'm not interested in any system", he once said, "I can't see any trace of any system anywhere." He is writing about waiting, about helplessness and about human frustration, all of which interest him deeply and all of which he can make us experience directly.

The great danger in seeking some non-existent meaning in Beckett's

30

plays is that we shall miss the experience that is actually there. To quote George Devine yet again:

> To approach Beckett openly we have to give up asking 'What is it meant to mean?' with the kind of panic which leads to rejection or scorn. The short answer can only be, 'It means what it says'. Or, as a dramatist once replied to a journalist who asked him to define in a sentence what his play was about: 'If I could tell you in a sentence I wouldn't have written the play.'

Beckett himself, when Alan Schneider asked him who or what Godot means, answered quite simply, "If I knew, I would have said so in the play." Had he done so, the play would have been something radically different.

During a conversation in 1956, Beckett suggested that the early success of *Waiting for Godot* was based on a fundamental misunderstanding, critics and public alike insisting on interpreting in allegorical or symbolical terms a play which was striving all the time to avoid definition. This avoidance of definition is implicit in Beckett's work, for if each member of an audience is to respond out of himself, he must not be arbitrarily inhibited by the dramatist. To give an example, had Beckett told us that the scene in *Waiting for Godot* is a deserted country road in County Dublin, he would have been restricting us by making us think of one definite place to the exclusion of all other country roads. A Frenchman, knowing nothing of Ireland, might become uncomfortable fearing that he was missing some vital allusion, while a County Dublin man might concentrate excessively on the accuracy of Beckett's local colour. In each, the freedom of response would have been restricted; each could have missed the essential experience and to no purpose. In fact it makes no difference where the action is set; what matters is the waiting. Therefore Beckett simply says *a country road* and we think of it where it is most real to each one of us. It could be anywhere, equally well nowhere in particular; Beckett leaves us complete freedom of reaction. Proust says that every time we write a sentence we take an idea prisoner, and Beckett would doubtless agree that every specific detail lessens the potential truth of a work of art. An example from grammar may make this point clearer. An adjective can be described as a word which tells us more about a noun, but it can be defined with equal accuracy as a word which qualifies a noun, i.e. restricts its application. If we say that a book is blue we know more about one particular book but we are limiting the number of books under consideration.

31

Beckett's method in all his plays is to qualify as little as possible and therefore to reduce the specific to a minimum. We have seen that by their very nature the plays can have no single, definite meaning. In the same way, and for the same reason, they must have the minimum of plot and characterisation. When a playwright tells us what happens next, he is inhibiting our response in exactly the same way as he does when he postulates where it happens. Whereas the conventional dramatist shows us a sequence of events or the resolution of some problem, Beckett presents us with situations as static as he can make them. To hope for any story in his work is as profitable as to hope for any specific message; as Winnie says in *Happy Days*: "Yes, something seems to have occurred, something has seemed to occur, and nothing has occurred, nothing at all, . . ." *Waiting for Godot* begins and ends with two men waiting for night to fall or for Godot to come. The most we can say of the action is that time has moved imperceptibly forward. In *Endgame* there is waiting also; a blind tyrant spins an interminable story as he waits, for death, perhaps, or for his servant to leave him. When the curtain falls he is still alive and the servant stands watching him from a threshold which he has not crossed. With Hamm and Clov, as with Vladimir and Estragon, to-morrow may well be this same day. *Krapp's Last Tape* shows us an old man failing to achieve a statement, or to be more precise, failing to make a tape recording; we leave him motionless staring before him as the tape runs on in silence. In *Happy Days*, Winnie is trying to pass the time between waking and sleeping as pleasantly as possible in a world where the opportunities for physical movement, let alone for diversion, are steadily diminishing. In *Play*, the protagonists, two women and a man, each imprisoned up to the neck in an urn, soliloquize in a hellish half-light.

Occasionally we may be faced with some obvious alteration on the stage. In *Godot*, for example, a tree sprouts leaves overnight and in *Happy Days*, Winnie, at first buried to her waist, is later found embedded to her neck. These changes take place between the acts and no explanation for them is ever offered. They do not produce a new situation; they simply underline the old one. The tree may sprout, but Godot has not come although he has promised to do so to-night. Winnie can no longer count on external objects to help her pass the time, she must draw more and more upon herself. The changes are stage facts, important only in the way in which the protagonists react to them. Of themselves they have no other meaning or significance and Beckett has no other interest in them. We are on the wrong tack if we try to read into them anything more than we are told. In a letter to Alan Schneider, dated 12 August, 1957, Beckett wrote:

> It would be impertinent for me to advise you about the article you are doing and I don't intend to. But when it comes to journalists I feel the only line is to refuse to be involved in exegesis of any kind. And to insist on the extreme simplicity of dramatic situation and issue. If that's not enough for them, and it obviously isn't, it's plenty for us, and we have no elucidations to offer of mysteries that are all of their making. My work is a matter of fundamental sounds (no joke intended) made as fully as possible, and I accept responsibility for nothing else. If people want to have headaches among the overtones, let them. And provide their own aspirin. Hamm as stated, and Clov as stated, together as stated, nec tecum nec sine te, in such a place, and in such a world, that's all I can manage, more than I could.

"Hamm as stated, and Clov as stated . . . . in such a place, and in such a world, that's all I can manage, more than I could." Here we come to another distinctive feature of Beckett's plays. His protagonists, his "people", as he calls them, exist and can exist only for as long as the play lasts, indeed only for as long as they are before our eyes. Beckett gives us no hint as to how they have come to the situation in which we find them. They have no past except for what they may tell us, and no future. At the end of the play, they will be virtually unchanged. When a very eminent actor who was thinking of playing Pozzo in the West End asked Beckett for details of the character's age, nationality, education, financial background and so on, Beckett, usually the most obliging of men, could not provide these details because he literally did not know them and he was too honest to concoct an answer. On another occasion an American journalist asked him if he had no interest in economics; did he never treat problems such as how his characters earned their living? "My characters have nothing," Beckett said, and then, in the words of the journalist, "let the matter drop." One cannot help recalling the reply of the elderly actor, once a celebrated Hamlet, when asked by a young man about to play the part for the first time if the Prince slept with Ophelia, "In my day, my boy, invariably".

The story serves to illustrate the wrong-headedness of the American's question, but it also reminds us of the adjustment which is needed in our attitude to Beckett's plays. Many people complain that they are sordid, repetitive, meaningless, have no story, have none of the glitter which we associate with the word theatrical, above all that they have no relation to life as we know it. This last objection is partially valid. We do not normally find people who keep their parents in dustbins, as in *Endgame,* nor do we come across well-preserved ladies of about fifty, blonde for preference, buried to their waists or to their necks in mounds of earth under a blazing sky as we do in *Happy Days.* But the criticism misses the essential point that Beckett is not concerned with reproducing what we call life as we know it. As he says, he is trying to chart a whole zone of being in the individual, hitherto left severely alone by the artist. To conduct these little explorations, as he calls them, he has evolved this special kind of play, based on impact not argument, striving all the time to avoid definition — a kind of play which for our purposes we shall call the drama of the non-specific. Our next step will be to look closely at one of these non-specific dramas, *Play,* to see how it works in the theatre and then to consider some reactions to it. By so doing, it is hoped, we may come nearer to that open approach needed to appreciate this new form of art. Then we will consider a second play, *Waiting for Godot,* to see if we can understand a little more clearly how this new drama of the non-specific as created by Beckett breaks fresh ground, and how it has enlarged the range of the theatre.

Towards an Open Approach

When working as a director on a Beckett play (and this is my third production) one has to think of the text as something like a musical score wherein the "notes", the sights, the sounds, the pauses, have their own special inter-related rhythms, and out of their composition comes the dramatic impact.

(Programme note by George Devine to the National Theatre production of *Play,* at the Old Vic, London, April 7th, 1964.)

One glance at the published text of *Play* suffices to show the truth of George Devine's comparison of it to a musical score. Just as the composer gives precise instructions to the conductor and musicians as to how his work is to be played, so Beckett gives precise instructions to the director and the actors as to how this play is to be set, lighted and spoken. Any departure from these instructions by either actor or producer would amount to a distortion of the work, just as any departure from the score by a conductor or a musician would be a distortion of what the composer had created.

There are only three *dramatis personae* in *Play*, and they have no names, being simply designated in the text and on the programme as First Woman (w1), Second Woman (w2), and Man (m). No indications are given as to place or time; Beckett sets his stage as follows:

> Front centre, touching one another, three identical grey urns about one yard high. From each a head protrudes, the neck held fast in the urn's mouth. The heads are those, from left to right as seen from auditorium, of w2, m and w1. They face undeviatingly front throughout the play. Faces so lost to age and aspect as to seem almost part of urns. But no masks.

At the end of the text Beckett provides the following note:

> In order for the urns to be only one yard high, it is necessary either that traps be used, enabling the actors to stand below stage level, or that they kneel throughout the play, the urns being open at the back.
>
> Should traps be not available, and the kneeling posture found impracticable, the actors should stand, the urns be enlarged to full length and moved back from front to mid-stage, the tallest actor setting the height, the broadest the breadth, to which the three urns should conform.
>
> The sitting posture results in urns of unacceptable bulk and is not to be considered.

The characters are in urns because they are dead; they face "undeviatingly front throughout the play" because the neck of each is "held fast in the urn's mouth", i.e., each is literally contained by an urn. Thus there can be no change of position, no movement which might bring relaxation to the actors or distraction to us. "The faces so lost to age and aspect as to seem almost part of urns" make it impossible for us to graft upon them any definite identity which we may have thought up. Yet they have "no masks" because this is a play about human beings. On these three faces our entire attention will be fixed throughout the play since, apart from the urns, there is nothing else for us to look at. By an apparently wanton sacrifice of colour, movement and change — three of the dramatist's major assets — Beckett achieves a fantastic degree of concentration inducing a heightened awareness — the very essence of the dramatic experience.

Their speech is provoked by a spotlight projected on faces alone.

In another note at the end of the text, Beckett is more precise about this spot:

LIGHT

The source of light is single and must not be situated outside the ideal space (stage) occupied by its victims. The optimum position for the spot is at the centre of the footlights, the faces being thus lit at close quarters and from below.

When exceptionally three spots are required to light the three faces simultaneously, they should be as a single spot branching into three.

Apart from these moments a single mobile spot should be used, swivelling at maximum speed from one face to another as required

The method consisting in assigning to each face a separate fixed spot is unsatisfactory in that it is less expressive of a unique inquisitor than the single mobile spot.

From this it is obvious that Beckett is using the spotlight not just to illuminate the faces of the actors; it is a character as much as its victims and so it is on stage with them. In performance this is tremendously effective, though curiously enough we are never tempted to try to find any explanation for the light. The constantly swivelling beam gives the sense of movement which the actors in their urns cannot; at the same time it intensifies the concentration, producing a strong sense of claustrophobia.

The transfer of light from one face to another is immediate. No blackout, i.e., return to almost complete darkness of opening, except where indicated.

The response to light is not quite immediate. At every solicitation a pause of about one second before utterance is achieved, except where a longer delay is indicated.

The length of every blackout is indicated by Beckett; some last five seconds, some three. As in a conventional play, the extinction of light suggests a break. The longer blackouts mark a change in direction, while the shorter seem to suggest a momentary stumble.

> Faces impassive throughout. Voices toneless except where an expression is indicated.
> Rapid tempo throughout.

The toneless voices and the rapid tempo serve three purposes. They make it impossible for the actor or director to import any personal interpretation of the rôles over and above what Beckett has provided; there can be no question of the performance being "true to life" beyond the given situation. Secondly, and as a result of the first voluntary limitation, the audience are compelled to concentrate on what is coming at them instead of indulging in fantasies of their own. Thirdly, because the tempo and the tonelessness are not already familiar, the audience must grow accustomed to them, thereby increasing their awareness — a vital part of the experience which Beckett is presenting.

> The curtain rises on a stage in almost complete darkness. Urns just discernible. Five seconds.
> Faint spots simultaneously on three faces. Three seconds. Voices faint, largely unintelligible.

The spot is faint and the voices are faint because something is moving towards us; we have not been plunged *in media res*. As sound and light become stronger, the sense of immediacy likewise is strengthened. The words, which Beckett in a note refers to as the Chorus, and which he sets out in parts like a musical score, are "largely unintelligible" not only because the characters are speaking different lines all at once, thereby jamming each other, but also because at this point the words themselves have no context; we have no idea what they could possibly be. This will not always be so.

After the Chorus, roughly 45 words from each speaker, there is another long blackout. Then the spot comes on again, still branching into three and illuminating all the characters, but it is now strong, and when, after a three-second pause, the characters speak, their voices are at "normal strength". Simultaneously they start to deliver new opening lines but, after roughly six words, there is another blackout; after five seconds the spot returns, this time single, and picks out w1 who speaks uninterrupted. Henceforth, for 32 speeches and about 1,020 words in which the situation unfolds, the spot will stay single, extracting speech from one victim at a time, hitting now one, now another. The overture has ended and the narrative can begin.

By this time, the audience is bewildered but curious, anxious to know what is going on. This knowledge comes piecemeal. The subsequent speeches are closely related, but since the characters believe themselves to be alone, and are conscious of nothing but the enveloping darkness and the probing spot, this relationship cannot be the usual one of statement and reply or question and answer. Rather, each speech is like a piece of a jig-saw puzzle, almost meaningless of itself but acquiring increased significance when fitted to another to which it, likewise, gives added meaning. The points of connection between one utterance and those around it, either preceding or succeeding it, are easily recognized. We have only to look at the first half-dozen speeches to see how the links are made.

w1 : I said to him, Give her up. I swore by all I held most sacred—
Spot from w1 to w2.

w2 : One morning as I was sitting stitching by the open window she burst in and flew at me. Give him up, she screamed, he's mine. Her photographs were kind to her. Seeing her now for the first time full length in the flesh I understood why he preferred me.
Spot from w2 to m.

m : We were not long together when she smelled the rat. Give up that whore, she said, or I'll cut my throat — (*hiccup*)* pardon — so help me God. I knew she could have no proof. So I told her I did not know what she was talking about.
Spot from m to w2.

w2 : What are you talking about? I said, stitching away. Someone

---

*This hiccup is a stage direction, as much part of the text as the words and phrases. m hiccups five times at points determined by Beckett, not the director. The hiccup prevents m ever becoming heroic.

yours? Give up whom? I smell you off him, she screamed, he stinks of bitch.

Spot from w2 *to* w1.

w1 : Though I had him dogged for months by a first-rate man, no shadow of proof was forthcoming. And there was no denying that he continued as . . . assiduous as ever. This, and his horror of the merely Platonic thing, made me sometimes wonder if I were not accusing him unjustly. Yes.

Spot from w1 *to* m.

m : What have you to complain of? I said. Have I been neglecting you? How could we be together in the way we are if there were someone else? Loving her as I did, with all my heart, I could not but feel sorry for her.

w1 and m are obviously describing the same thing, a bitter quarrel over another woman. m's account of the conversation, "Give up that whore, she said, or I'll cut my throat—(*hiccup*) pardon—so help me God" is in ironic contrast to w1's dignified, "I said to him, Give her up. I swore by all I held most sacred —" but the incident itself is unmistakable. Between these two speeches, w2 describes how a hysterical woman had burst in upon her screaming "Give him up". The repetition of the phrase enables us to recognize the intruder as w1, while "he's mine" establishes The Eternal Triangle and the respective positions of the two women in it. m in turn confirms the liaison and the quarrel, at the same time preparing the way for the next speech.

The points of intersection are not established by incident alone. There is a kind of verbal telepathy binding the three speakers together. m's speech ends, "I told her I did not know what she was talking about." This is immediately echoed by w2's "What are you talking about? I said . . .". Again, m had previously said, "I knew she could have no proof", w2 reports that w1 had screamed, "He stinks of bitch". These are fused and echoed by w1 herself, "Though I had him *dogged* (italics mine) for months by a first-rate man, no shadow of *proof* (italics mine) was forthcoming . . .". By these repetitions and variations—variations which by their very existence postulate a theme —Beckett clips three fractions into a unity. As the spot probes, the story, everyday as it is, unfolds, and the characters, commonplace as they are, establish themselves. The spot seems to follow no discernible pattern as it jerks our eyes and our attention from one urn to another in no predictable sequence. Herein lies much of the initial suspense which is heightened as we begin to piece the clues together, experiencing all the excitement of things hitherto mysterious falling into place. On first hearing the play we get the impression that each character says about the same amount, and a check with the text confirms this. There are roughly 150 words more in the longest part (w2) than in the shortest (w1).

Although the narratives clearly interlock, they do not begin at the same point or move at the same speed; w2 tends to be slightly ahead of the others. If we put the events down in chronological sequence, however, we get something like this. m, a married man, and w2 have been carrying on a love affair but before long m's wife, w1, becomes suspicious. She accuses m who denies everything. w1 threatens to kill herself. She then calls on w2, tells her to give m up and threatens to kill her. w2 likewise denies all knowledge of the affair and has w1 shown out by her servant. w1 then hires a private detective to shadow m but no evidence is forthcoming because m, realizing what is happening, bribes the detective. All this time, as w1 admits, m has been as "assiduous" as ever to her, and this he cites as proof of his fidelity, an argument she accepts knowing "his horror of the merely Platonic thing". When m complains to w2 of his life at home, she urges him to leave w1 since there is no longer anything between them, "Or", she asks, "is there?" m, righteously indignant, denies even the possibility of such a thing — does she take him for "a something machine?" — an argument she accepts since "with him no danger of . . . the spiritual thing". Suddenly m's nerve snaps and he confesses to w1 who, according to him, has been looking more and more desperate and has been carrying a razor in her bag. w1 forgives him, "to what will love not stoop?" and suggests a little jaunt abroad to celebrate. This is not immediately possible because of m's "professional commitments". Satisfied that m is now all hers, w1 again calls on w2 to gloat over her; w2 once more has her shown out, and when m next visits w2, she tries to end the affair. As she says, she has no silly threats to offer, but not much stomach for another woman's leavings either. m insists that he cannot live without w2 and agrees that the thing is to go away together though this is not immediately possible until m has "put his affairs in order". They decide to carry on as before. A period of domestic bliss follows for m, unbroken even when w1 tells him that she has met his "ex-doxy", and that he is "well out of that". "Rather uncalled-for, I thought. I am, indeed, sweetheart, I said. I am indeed. God what vermin women. Thanks to you angel . . ." But w1 soon becomes suspicious again and m, feeling that it is "all too much", disappears. "I simply could no longer . . . .", the sentence remains unfinished. w1, now believing that m's disappearance means victory for w2, lies stricken for weeks, then drives over to her rival's house only to find it shut up. On the way back "by Ash and Snodland . . . .", this sentence also remains unfinished. w2 says that when m stopped coming, i.e., after his disappearance, she was prepared "more or less". She made a bundle of his things and burnt them. "It was November and the bonfire was going. All night I smelt them smouldering". Here, suddenly without explanation, the probing spotlight is switched off and there is a blackout. After five seconds the spot, now forked and at half strength, comes on, falling on all three as at the beginning of the play. The voices are "proportionately lower" and the three characters simultaneously speak two or three words, their first lines in this, the second section of the play. Again the spot goes off, there is a blackout for five seconds, then the single spot picks out one character, this time m, who proceeds uninterrupted.

From m's opening words, "When first this change I actually thanked God", we know that we have entered upon a new phase. The shift is from narrative to reflection, the spot now evoking feelings or fantasies, not facts. There are still occasional verbal echoes but the utterances do not intersect so closely or so often. This part of the play is, therefore, more difficult to describe, for the characters, no longer telling of their inter-reactions, speak more from themselves, and there is no finite event like a quarrel or a reconciliation towards which the words can be orientated. In contrast to the close-knit conflict of the first phase, we now get a sense of disintegration. The speeches are much shorter; the light shifts more often. It probes and the characters speak; no other sequence is discernible.

Certain themes occupy the protagonists, but the treatments come in no apparent order, are not connected with each other, and form no pattern — save perhaps one of flux. All three comment on their changed situation, speculate about the other two, pity them, and wonder about their own relationship with the ceaselessly jabbing spot. They seem to drift between spells of acute suffering and comparatively tolerable periods — as w2 says, "there are endurable moments". But there is no undeviating movement, no steadily rising crescendo of pain or knowledge. Bathos succeeds anguish, perception is followed by triviality, w1, for example, realizes that her mind cannot accept the possibility that "There is no sense in this . . . . either, none whatsoever". "And that all is falling, all fallen, from the beginning, on empty air. Nothing being asked at all. No one asking me for anything at all". From this abyss of nothingness she turns quickly to a reminiscence of w2. "She had means, I fancy, though she lived like a pig". Similarly m admits quite early on "I know now all that was just . . . play", and goes on to ask "All this, when will all this have been . . . just play?" But he immediately drops this question, to indulge in a smug fantasy picturing the two women drinking tea. "Perhaps sorrow has brought them together", — sorrow, that is, because they have lost him.

So the ebb and flow continues, the same expressionless voices speaking at the same rapid tempo as the spot switches tirelessly from urn to urn, cutting short every utterance when it withdraws, eliciting speech when it arrives. Once, after the forty-seventh move of the spot, something different happens. w2 is speaking, "Like dragging a great roller, on a scorching day. The strain . . . to get it moving, momentum coming —" Here the spot goes out and w2 falls silent, but instead of the light fixing immediately on w1 or m, there is a blackout of three seconds. For the first time since this reflective section began, the stage is in darkness and total silence; there is a definite stumble. The spot comes on again, still on w2 who says, "Kill it and strain again". The spot withdraws, she stops, and we continue as before with the familiar routine of spot selecting its victim, first victim speaking, spot moving to second victim, first victim falling silent, second victim beginning to speak. There has been a jolt, no more, and it is hard to see that any development is possible in this flux.

Yet development comes and with devastating effect. Quite early in this second section, twenty-six spot moves before the jolt, w2 had been talking half to herself, half to the light, "You might get angry and blaze me clean out of my wits, mightn't you?"—an idea which at that point she abandons, "But I doubt it. It would not be like you somehow". Twelve moves after the stumble, she has returned to this possibility of madness, "Am I not a little unhinged already?" When the spot fixes on her next, four moves later, she repeats her question and adds *hopefully* — one of Beckett's two explicit directions on tone of voice. — "Just a little. (*Pause.*) I doubt it." Five moves further on, the idea is still there, "A shade gone. In the head. Just a shade. I doubt it". Four moves afterwards comes the climax. The light falls on her, "*I doubt it. Pause. Peal of wild low laughter from* w2 *cut short as spot from her to* w1". This laughter is in shattering contrast to the swift, expressionless tempo of the past quarter of an hour. We have heard it once before, but have probably forgotten it; it was part of the Chorus with which the play began. When next the beam picks out w2 five moves subsequently she says nothing; there is only *"laugh as before"*, cut short as the spot switches from her to m.

m, meanwhile, is moving towards the question, "Am I as much as being seen?" an idea already turned over by w1 and w2. In the middle of this he is interrupted by a blackout of three seconds, a second jolt. The spot returns to him, however, he finishes his question, but the probing does not continue. Instead there is a blackout lasting five seconds — the sign of a break in the action as distinct from a jolt or falter — and when the spot comes on again, it is dim, three-pronged, falling on all three actors. There is a pause of three seconds, then they begin to speak that "largely unintelligible" Chorus with which the play had opened. We have come full circle: here Beckett's stage direction reads *"Repeat play exactly"*.

This presents no difficulties for a well-drilled cast and a competent director, but for the audience the effect of this identical repeat must be very different from that of the original performance. Already at this second hearing the "largely unintelligible" words of the Chorus are less unintelligible because now they have acquired context. We have heard them, or something very like them, spoken singly and intelligibly by one actor or another during the reflective phase which has just ended, and w2's laugh is terrifyingly familiar. We may perhaps recognize the second, shorter burst of Chorus as the first words of each player in the opening narrative section. Even if we do not immediately analyse the Chorus, our reactions to the whole narrative section must be quite different. Whereas during the first hearing we were bewildered and curious, we now know all about the love affair and what is in store for the three protagonists. This increased knowledge involves us. If we are not actually in hell, purgatory, limbo or whatever else we call this region of half-light, we are a great deal nearer to it than we were. But our experience and our journey do not stop here. For a second time we go through it all, see w2's mind snap and experience the jolt as m is halted by the three-second blackout in the middle of his final question. But what will happen next? Suddenly we realize that perhaps we must go through the whole experience yet a third time with our nerves now bare, our awareness almost intolerably heightened by the repetition we have just been through. It is as if we are lying stretched on a rack waiting for another turn of the screw. m finishes his question, "Am I as much as . . . . being seen?" Again the blackout for five seconds, now followed by a terrifying variation. Instead of the faint triple spot and the largely unintelligible Chorus with which the play has started twice already, the light falls on all three and together they speak their first words of the narrative section. We are back at the beginning, still moving over the same ground but infinitesimally faster. Again a five-second blackout and the spot returns at full strength falling on only one character, m this time, not w1, a change perhaps but no significant development, for once again m speaks his opening line, "We were not long together . . ." The spot goes off, m falls silent, there is a blackout of five seconds—agonizing for those who are thinking of what may lie ahead—then the final curtain falls. All this has taken roughly forty minutes, or about the same time as from the curtain rise to the first interval of a conventional three-act play. The text, if we ignore the repetition, runs to just over 2,250 words, the equivalent of six pages in this book or about three in a glossy magazine; the longest single speech takes a little more than twenty seconds. So much for the play, but what of its impact?

Professor Hugh Kenner has described the situations presented by Beckett as existing at such a level of simplicity that one can, indeed, say of them all that can be said. This is surely true of *Play*. There is nothing which leaves the slightest room for argument over its interpretation since, as George Devine says, "The story and dialogue are of a deliberately banal order." Yet, for all its simplicity, *Play* produced widely differing reactions. To the present writer, who saw Devine's production in London, it brought an agony of heightening awareness, accompanied by a correspondingly heightened understanding. Barbara Bray, who reviewed the world première at Ulm for *The Observer*, found truths but no statements: "these three suffering heads conjure up not only three whole lives, but also awaken the reverberations that transform them from the trivial to the universal. Here are people in all their funny, disgraceful, pitiable fragility, and all the touchingness, in spite of everything, of their efforts to love one another, and endure". Earlier she had remarked, "The play ends on an infinite echo, with the re-commencement of the man's story: 'We were not long together'." George Devine describes an audience in front of *Play* as "invited to undergo an experience. It may be a strange one, an unusual one, even a nerve-racking one, but taken rightly it will be a dramatic one by a profound and brilliant poet of the theatre."

These three reactions complement each other, interlocking like the speeches in *Play*. The heightened awareness has come from submitting ourselves to a dramatic experience prepared by a profound and brilliant poet of the theatre, an experience which has induced in us reverberations able to transform the trivial into the universal. This universal, the aim of the artist, be he poet, sculptor, musician, painter, novelist, dramatist, lies in truths not statements. "Beauty is truth, truth beauty".

Not everyone, however, reacts to *Play* in this way. The drama critic of *Time Magazine* who attended the same performance as Miss Bray felt very differently:

> Each time a Samuel Beckett play has a world premiêre, the world turns a deeper shade of black. Once his people were hopefully waiting for *Godot;* later they crouched in garbage cans in *Endgame;* Krapp was moribund while listening to his last tape; then in *Happy Days,* the female lead kept sinking deeper and deeper into a mound. Now Beckett's characters have gone all the way to hell in a play called *Play,* which has just opened in West Germany.
>
> Only the heads of the three actors could be seen. Their bodies were inside giant clay urns. Spotlights kept picking out the appropriate urn as the dialogue developed like this:
>
> 'Puffy face, tits, hanging cheeks, false blond. I can't understand why he went for her. He had me.'
>
> 'Ha ha ha ha. Can you see me? Why can't I be seen in this muddy light of hell?'
>
> 'We were all together (*burp*), pardon me, for such a short time.'
>
> Unlike Sartre's *No Exit,* where hell becomes a perpetuation of emotions suffered in life, Beckett's *Play* presents its posthumans as essentially bored, driven solely by an excessive urge to repeat themselves, as they gradually spill out what proves to be a conventional story about a man, his wife and his mistress. The urge is so strong, in fact, that the second half of the play is a verbatim recapitulation of the first half. Nonetheless, at the opening night curtain, a scattering of hisses and boos was obliterated by eager applause.

This fourth reaction deserves careful study, for it, too, has much to tell us. The writer does not for one moment entertain the possibility that he might be watching a new kind of play or that any adjustment might be necessary if he is to enjoy it or even to criticize it. He makes no mention of the piece's obvious peculiarities — the suppression of all personal details, the expressionless voices, or the unchanging, rapid tempo at which the lines are spoken. He misunderstands the purpose of the spot, and interprets the repetition of the play in terms which he himself imports but which were never used or hinted at by the author. The contrast with *No Exit* is especially interesting. By referring to this play, the writer implies that both Sartre and Beckett are trying to do more or less the same thing, to offer us some ideas on the nature of Hell. Otherwise the contrast has no point. But this is not so. No two plays could be more unlike than Sartre's precisely-drawn, exciting, psychological study with its neat capsule summary "Hell is other people", and Beckett's deliberately vague, repetitive, inconclusive piece ending on an infinite echo. Sartre provides a definite story and advances a definite argument; Beckett reduces story to its very minimum and avoids anything even remotely resembling a conclusion. The contrast drawn by the *Time* drama critic is, then, irrelevant and the very fact that it should have been attempted shows how far he was out of touch with what he had seen, shows too how he is importing his own preconceived ideas instead of submitting himself to the experience.

It must be admitted that the great majority of theatre-goers unfamiliar with Beckett's distinctive technique would sympathize with the *Time* correspondent. Until Beckett's method and purpose are understood, until we make the necessary adjustment, we are all likely to experience bewilderment, incredulity, anger or contempt. The characters seem so outrageous, the situations so fantastic that we instinctively react in the same way as the French philosopher shown an elephant for the first time, "I don't believe it".

This elephant epitomizes our argument. Without exception Beckett's plays are as different from conventional plays as elephant is from all trunkless animals. As long as we deny elephant's existence, or insist on regarding him as a trunkless animal gone wrong, we are no wiser for having seen him. We have failed to assimilate him. Elephant needs no interpretation; he is simply there for us to take or to leave. So are Beckett's plays. As trunk is the distinctive feature of elephant, so impact is the distinctive feature of Beckett's work. This impact is produced by something more than story or argument, and it is not confined to the intellect. Beckett's concern is with situations, not stories, anguish not argument, truth not statements, and truths of the kind with which the artist rather than the mathematician is familiar. As another Irishman, the poet Louis MacNeice, wrote of his wife:

47

"Whose kaleidoscopic ways are all authentic,
    Whose truth is not of a statement but of a dance
So that even when you deceive your deceits are merely
    Technical and of no significance.
And so, when I think of you, I have to meet you
    In thought on your own ground;
To apply to you my algebraic canons
    Would merely be unsound . . . ."

There are no deceits with Beckett any more than with elephant, and, if we are to enjoy his plays, it is essential that we try to meet him on his own ground. There is nothing unreasonable about this. Brendan Behan summed it up in three simple sentences: "I don't know what his (Beckett's) plays are about, but I do know I enjoy them. I do not know what a swim in the ocean is about, but I enjoy it. I enjoy the water flowing over me". If by now we are nearer to recognizing the need for the open approach, then elephant and *Play* have served their purpose.

An Art of Love

This man (Beckett) seemed to have lived and suffered so that I could see, and he was generous enough to pass it on to me.

George Devine.

Before we examine *Waiting for Godot* as an example of how Beckett has changed and enlarged the theatre, we must remind ourselves that *Godot* is an outstandingly successful play. Since its première in Paris on January 5th, 1953, it has been performed by all sorts of actors in all sorts of places, by negroes in Harlem, by convicts in a German prison, by pupils of Beckett's old school in the North of Ireland. It has been played in more than twenty different countries from Finland to the Argentine, and has been translated into at least fifteen different languages, as different as Serbo-Croat and Japanese. Clearly we are not dealing with a play of limited appeal, or, as many insist, with an elaborate intellectual hoax. *Godot* has turned out to be world theatre.

No one could have been more surprised at this than the author. At their first meeting Beckett told his director, Roger Blin, that he confidently expected *Godot* to play to almost empty houses, probably, as he added, the ideal conditions for it, and ninety-nine people out of a hundred would agree. It is hard to imagine anything less likely to prove an international success, a play in which as the critic Vivian Mercier says, "Nothing happens, *twice*." There is no story, no "message", no spectacle, no star part, no sex, not even a woman in the cast. Why, then, has it succeeded? Why does it still succeed, and why has it become widely recognized as possibly the most important play of the last fifty years? These questions are hard to answer, but a remark of Tyrone Guthrie's provides a good starting point for our investigations. "Take a situation of general human application," he once said, "charge it with the overtones of myth, and no wise man will refuse to listen to you."

At first sight *Godot* would seem to bear scant reference to the human predicament. We feel little inclination to identify ourselves with these garrulous unkempt vagabonds indifferent to all the concerns of civilized life as we know it. Even if we were so tempted, Beckett has deliberately withheld every detail that would make this possible. Godot sounds as if he might have some significance; but a glance at the programme tells us that he will not appear. If, however, we forget about the civilized world for a moment, close our programmes, and simply watch what is happening on the stage, we will realize that Vladimir and Estragon, or Didi and Gogo as they call each other, are waiting, and that the waiting is of a particular kind.

They are not like men at the proper stop, expecting a bus which they know will come at a fixed time or within a given period. They may say they are waiting for Godot, but they cannot say who or what he is, nor can they be sure that they are at the right place, or if it is the right day, or what will happen when Godot comes, or what would happen if they gave up waiting. Their position more closely resembles that of travellers miles from home waiting late at night at what could be the right or the wrong stop for the last bus which may already have gone anyway. They cannot be sure because they have no watches, no timetables, and there is no one from whom they can get information. Possibly they are at the wrong stop but could still catch the bus if they knew where to go; on the other hand, perhaps they are at the right stop and still in time, but if they move, the bus may come and go without them. Maybe the bus has already gone, and by remaining they are jeopardising their chances of finding a taxi, and all to no purpose. If only they were sure they could decide what was the best course open to them; but they cannot get the essential knowledge — they are ignorant — and without it they cannot act — they are impotent.

We are all familiar with the sense of baffled helplessness which comes welling up in us when we are forced to remain in an obscure situation over which we have no control. We know it, for instance, as we sit in an airport lounge hoping the fog will soon clear, as we watch the post for a love letter or for news of a job, as we wonder when the hospital will have something to tell us. The greater our fears or frustrations, the more eagerly we look for some means of taking our minds off things, some way to make the time pass more quickly. Almost anything will serve, however trivial, provided it helps to fill the vacuum, if only for a few minutes.

This is exactly what Estragon and Vladimir are doing from the beginning of the play. They tell stories, sing songs, play verbal games, pretend to be Pozzo and Lucky, do their physical exercises, but all these are mere stop-gaps, valuable only to occupy the twenty-four hours that must separate one possible meeting with Godot from the next. They understand this perfectly. "Come on Gogo", pleads Didi, breaking off a reflection on the two thieves crucified with Christ, "return the ball, can't you, once in a way?" and Estragon does; as he says later, "We don't manage too badly, eh Didi, between the two of us," .... "We always find something, eh Didi, to give us the impression we exist." Here we have the very essence of boredom — actions repeated long after the reason for them has been forgotten, and talk, purposeless of itself, but invaluable as a way to kill time.

We are fast approaching the heart of the matter, the crux of *Godot*.

The poet Bryan Guinness speaks of art as that magic which enables us to see with another man's eyes, feel with another man's heart, without recourse to the roundabout method of description. Beckett himself has said of Joyce, "His writing is not *about* something; *it is that something itself,*" and this direct expression, as he calls it, this presentation of the thing itself as distinct from any description of it or statement about it, is what Beckett achieves in the theatre. *Waiting for Godot* is not about Godot or even about waiting. It *is* waiting, and ignorance, and impotence and boredom, all made visible and audible on the stage before us, direct expression to which we respond directly, if at all because in it we recognize our own experience. We may never have waited by a tree on a deserted country road for night to fall or for a distant acquaintance to keep his appointment, but we have sat in an airport lounge on a foggy day, we have watched the post, we have wondered when we would hear from the hospital — we have lived through these situations or innumerable others like them. So, after all, we find ourselves on common ground with Vladimir and Estragon; we feel with them and, as it seems, with millions of others, Finns and Argentines, Japanese and Serbs, with everyone who has known ignorance, impotence and boredom. Here is that situation of general human application postulated by Tyrone Guthrie. "I think," said Beckett in 1956, "anyone nowadays, who pays the slightest attention to his own experience finds it the experience of a non-knower, a non-can-er." (i.e. of someone ignorant, therefore impotent.) The history of *Godot* seems to bear him out.

Yet before Beckett, no one in the theatre had come to grips with this experience; indeed as long as the dramatist and the public thought along the traditional lines of a well-made play with a strong story involving conflict, character development and a final solution, nothing could be done with it. Impotence cannot produce action, and without action there can be neither conflict nor solution. The only possible character development for a non-knower is to turn him into a knower, thereby destroying him altogether. Movement, therefore, is clearly impossible, but, as was generally accepted in the theatre, *le mouvement, c'est la vie* — a static drama was a contradiction in terms. By substituting situation for story, and sensuous, direct impact for logical, indirect description, Beckett has cut through this difficulty and has bridged the gulf between a widely felt emotion and the expression of it on the stage. But he has done more than solve one specific artistic problem; he has in effect created a whole new concept of drama much as the Impressionists created a whole new concept of painting. Just as the artist who has grasped the Impressionist technique is not confined to painting only bridges or sunflowers, so the dramatist who has grasped this concept of direct expression through total theatre is not confined to working with ignorance and impotence. Beckett himself has applied it to time in at least three different ways, and to awareness, and James Saunders has made notable use of it in *Next Time I'll Sing To You*, where he brings it to bear on identity.

Beckett belongs to no school of dramatists, so current labels like The Theatre of Cruelty or The Theatre of the Absurd bear no relation to his work. Nor does he seem likely to found any school unless it be The Theatre of The Non . . . . His achievement can, perhaps, be gauged through a parallel with flying; with *Godot* we move from the age of the propeller aircraft into that of the jet. Range and power have been increased enormously and things cannot ever be quite the same again.

Beckett's own use of his discovery has been intensely personal. He does not relate it to any overall system of belief as a Marxist, an Existentialist, a Nihilist, or any other "ist" might do. The new kind of play which he has evolved directly serves his individual needs as a creative artist, and these needs are, he insists, strictly his own. He sees no evidence of any system anywhere, he has no message to give, yet he cannot escape an imperative urge to try to say the unsayable, if only to satisfy himself that he exists. In a very real sense, Beckett's is an art of involvement.

He does not, cannot, describe ignorance, impotence, with clinical detachment standing back as a doctor might noting symptoms, incidence, probable causes, effects, and possible cures. As he struggles to capture ignorance and impotence, he is tortured by these emotions himself. He is no Henry the Navigator sitting in his tower at Belem reading the reports of his captains; he is one of the captains actually on the deck, Vasco da Gama, say, or Columbus, as he rounds the last charted headland and goes on into the unknown, never sure of what lies ahead, or of whether he may not sail off the face of the earth altogether. Beckett has justly described himself as a man whose world has no outside; "It is impossible for me to talk about my writing because I am constantly working in the dark," he once explained, "it would be like an insect leaving his cocoon. I can only estimate my work from within." Hence, as Dan Davin puts it, in an article significantly entitled *Mr. Beckett's Everymen*, "It is his own feelings, his own life, he is directly expressing and not the lives of characters with whom we can be expected to identify ourselves."

The thing *itself* not something *about* the thing, creation not description, first hand not second, this is what makes *Godot* far more than a brilliantly original solution to a problem in play-writing. If it had only been a technical *tour de force* we could have treated it as such, arguing about it, analysing it, but never feeling it through our own experience. *Godot* springs directly from Beckett's own anguish — he has called it a howl — and we respond directly or not at all, because we, too, are human beings so made that we must feel as well as reason. Listen to Vladimir as he muses after Pozzo's final, terrible departure.

> VLADIMIR: Was I sleeping, while the others suffered? Am I sleeping now? Tomorrow, when I wake, or think I do, what shall I say of today? That with Estragon my friend, at this place, until the fall of night, I waited for Godot? That Pozzo passed, with his carrier, and that he spoke to us? Probably. But in all that what truth will there be? (ESTRAGON, *having struggled with his boots in vain, is dozing off again.* VLADIMIR *stares at him.*) He'll know nothing. He'll tell me about the blows he received and I'll give him a carrot. (*Pause.*) Astride of a grave and a difficult birth. Down in the hole, lingeringly, the grave-digger puts on the forceps. We have time to grow old. The air is full of our cries. (*He listens.*) But habit is a great deadener. (*He looks again at* ESTRAGON.) At me too someone is looking, of me too someone is saying, He is sleeping, he knows nothing, let him sleep on. (*Pause.*) I can't go on! (*Pause.*) What have I said?

He goes feverishly to and fro, halts finally at extreme left, broods.

Here creator and character are one. In his monograph on Proust, written over twenty years before *Godot*, Beckett had described "the perilous zones in the life of the individual, dangerous, precarious, painful, mysterious and fertile, when for a moment the boredom of living is replaced by the suffering of being." Now, before our eyes, Vladimir enters one such zone changing from clown into poet. He no longer feels any misery or anger on his own account. A few minutes earlier he had wakened Estragon for no better reason than that he was bored and frightened, but now as his awareness increases, Vladimir's concern goes beyond himself, beyond his friend, to embrace all sorts and conditions of men. Here is a piercing consciousness of the human condition, of the sadness implicit in being a living mortal. But there is

54

nothing deadening or paralysing about the suffering, quite the opposite, for as Beckett says, "it is the free play of every faculty." With this free play comes an end to self-deception. Vladimir had earlier admitted quite cheerfully that "The hours are long, under these conditions, and constrain us to beguile them with proceedings which—how shall I say —which may at first sight seem reasonable until they become a habit"; and as he says later, "habit is a great deadener." Now habit can no longer insulate him from the truth as with every faculty he feels the happenings of the day for what they are, a series of pathetic attempts to pass the time: "But in all that, what truth will there be?" Estragon, too, has suffered, and in the end what has he learned? "He'll know nothing. He'll tell me about the blows he received and I'll give him a carrot." Ignorance, impotence, remain unassailable; only time has passed imperceptibly. Vladimir now knows and accepts that life can be no more than the distance between birth and death, "Down in the hole, lingeringly, the gravedigger puts on the forceps. We have time to grow old." The lament is for all mankind, springing from a union of compassion and anguish as fundamental to Beckett's work as the sense of impotence and ignorance which directly inspires it. This anguish is not a thing of the intellect or of the body in isolation; it permeates the whole being as Beckett has already described in *Proust*. Marcel is waiting in his apartment for Albertine "whose non-arrival exalts a simple physical irritation into a flame of moral anguish, so that he listens for her step or for the sublime summons of the telephone not with his ear and mind, but with his heart." Such suffering transcends the immediate, and thus makes of Beckett's work, for all its savagery and irony, what one critic has called an art of goodwill, and another, an art of love.

At first sight this seems a strange claim. Physically, Beckett's people are nearly all repellent grotesques; Vladimir has bad breath and a weak bladder, Estragon's feet smell, Krapp is constipated, Willie can only crawl on all fours and eats his mucus, the man in *Play* suffers from flatulence, Nagg and Nell are toothless cripples, Hamm, a blind haemophiliac, cannot stand up, while Clov cannot sit down. Remarking on this pleasing circumstance, Hamm adds, "To every man his speciality," by which he means his deformity. Bereft of all physical dignity, Beckett's people have few pleasant character traits either, being, for the most part, cruel, violent, obscene, selfish, blasphemous, finding a corrosive pleasure in their own squalor and the abject helplessness of others. Krapp describes the world as "this old muckball" and life at sixty-nine as "the sour cud and the iron stool." Even Winnie, the gentlest of them, asks, "How can one better magnify the Almighty than by sniggering with him at his little jokes, particularly the poorer ones?" Nell is more direct. "Nothing", she says, "is funnier than unhappiness, I grant you that." Vladimir seems to speak for all of them when he refers to this "foul brood to which a cruel fate consigned us." The physical disgust, the savage irony, recall another Irishman — Jonathan Swift, but Beckett could never dissociate himself from his people as Swift does when he leaves Gulliver, still a man but now scarcely able to tolerate the society of his fellow humans, even that of his wife. "You're on earth," Hamm tells Clov, "there's no cure for that."

What cannot be cured must be endured, and in this process Beckett's people reveal unexpected virtues, charity, compassion, love, and an unbreakable determination to endure. Estragon, the smaller of the two though eager enough to die, will not hang himself first. Vladimir's greater weight might break the branch, leaving him to face the world alone. For his part, Vladimir is deeply protective, watching over Estragon as a fond parent watches over a sleeping child. For Winnie, the mere knowledge of Willie's proximity is adequate reason for going on, while a sound or even a sign from him is more than enough to make her day. Nagg and Nell, as eternally apart in their dustbins as the figures on the Grecian urn, speak a love duet heart-piercing in its tenderness. Even the nameless heads in *Play,* "emptied, ruined, impotent creatures", as *The Times* critic called them, can each feel pity and hope for the others, thus saving themselves from despair, and saving us with them. If pity and hope are possible in such a place, and in such a world, for such people, then they are possible anywhere for anyone, for us here. Nobody need be excluded. Beckett has reached rock-bottom, and, not very surprisingly, has revealed rock.

There is real comfort here; bed-rock may make a painful couch but at least one feels it, and by feeling knows that one is still alive. For Beckett the difference between life and death is absolute — to say one might as well be dead is as meaningful as to say that a girl is only a little bit pregnant — and this difference, true for everyone, everywhere, is established by suffering involving all our faculties. Only the dead do not feel, and in the whole of his work there is not one unfeeling man or woman. They all suffer, and their anguish, Beckett's anguish, finds an echo in us, becomes our anguish. Habit, as Vladimir says, is a great deadener, but anguish is a great reviver. As long as we stand aloof, we are certain to be bored, but the moment we sense that what Beckett is presenting corresponds to something in ourselves, that here, however improbably, is a part of our own lives, apathy is no longer possible. We feel and feel deeply, for Beckett does not deal in trifles. Furthermore, he is working from inside his material, and we have been drawn into it with him.

Each of us comes to Beckett by a different road because each of us has led a different life. Our discussion of *Godot* has included bus stops, airport lounges, love letters and hospitals — not one of which is mentioned in the play. These objects have not been used as symbols or metaphors; they stand for nothing beyond themselves. They have been introduced because, for the present writer, they occur in that area of his experience recognizable to him as the area of experience presented in *Godot*. Other people describe it differently. There is, for example, the cricketing enthusiast who likens *Godot* to waiting outside the Tavern at Lords for it to open — which it won't because the licence has been revoked — watching two deadly-dull batsmen but hoping that Sobers or Dexter will come in next — which they won't because they have gone home. One of the convicts in California said simply, "*Godot* is the outside." The Public Orator of Dublin University called it a modern equivalent of the Psalmist's *Expectans, Expectavi*. The cricketing enthusiast, as it happens, was an atheist, the convict had never seen a cricket match, and the professor had never been in prison, yet all three recognized the one experience — there is no divergence here like that separating the Roman Catholic critic and the Existentialist over the alleged meaning of *Godot*. Beckett's play is valid for cricketer, convict and professor alike because each is assimilating the general anguish into his particular experience and then translating it into his own terms. Without this process of assimilation the plays must be meaningless. *Play* can be only a gabble of words from a half-lit stage, *Krapp* the footlings of a constipated old man with a tape recorder, *Godot* the interminable complainings of what one early critic called Weary Willie and Tired Tim.

With assimilation, however, comes illumination. "The more I read Sam Beckett and feel his compassion for the human condition, I realize that the magnitude of my own youthful and harrowing problems need no longer be a tortured secret, but can really be understood and shared, and my existence made much more tolerable." These words were used in 1966 by a teenage girl, but Aristotle would instantly have recognized her experience as that process which about two thousand five hundred years ago he called catharsis. Nothing could seem further removed from classical Greek tragedy than these mutilated near-clowns of Beckett's, yet they work on us in the same way and produce the same effect as the Gods and Heroes of Aeschylus and Sophocles produced on their contemporaries. Through them we come to a clearer knowledge of ourselves, to an increased capacity to live fully, and so to a spiritual liberation. Beckett has restored the theatre to its classical function; in his hands it ceases to be a soporific and has become a stimulant; it is no longer an engine of escape, but a source of illumination.

PART TWO:
BECKETT'S DRAMATIC WORK

A Chronology
The Plays

A Chronology

This chronology records dates of composition of the work, perfor-
mances, and awards. It does not record details of publication. These
will be found in the section dealing with individual works.

1930 February 19. *Le Kid,* 'a Cornelian nightmare', presented at the
Peacock Theatre, Dublin, as one of three foreign plays staged
by the Dublin University Modern Languages Society.

1947 Writes *Eleutheria,* his first full-length play. Still unpublished
and unacted in 1967.

1948/1949
October to January. Writes *En Attendant Godot.*

1953 January 5. *En Attendant Godot* first produced at Théâtre de
Babylone, Paris.

1954 Translates *En Attendant Godot* into English.

1955 August 3. *Waiting for Godot* first produced at the Arts
Theatre Club, London. First production in English. Trans-
ferred to the Criterion Theatre, London, on September 12th.
October 28. *Waiting for Godot* produced at the Pike Theatre
Club, Dublin.

1956 January 3. *Waiting for Godot* opens at the Coconut Grove
Playhouse, Miami. First American production.
January. Beckett at work on a second play.
April 19. *Waiting for Godot* produced at the John Golden
Theatre, New York.
June 21. Beckett has finished *Fin de Partie.*
November 11. Beckett has finished *All That Fall,* a play for
radio, his first major dramatic work to be composed in English.

1957 January 13. *All That Fall* first broadcast, B.B.C. London
April 3. *Fin de Partie* and the mime *Acte Sans Paroles I*
produced at the Royal Court Theatre, London. World première
in French.

April 26. *Fin de Partie* produced at Studio des Champs Elysées, Paris. First production in France.

April 30 to August 12. Translates *Fin de Partie* into English and calls it *Endgame*.

December 14. Patrick Magee 'speaks' *From an Abandoned Work* on B.B.C. London.

1958   January. Disagreement in progress with the Lord Chamberlain over *Endgame*.

January 28. *Endgame* produced at Cherry Lane Theatre, New York. World première in English.

February. Disagreement with Dublin Theatre Festival. Beckett withdraws three mimes probably including *Act Without Words II* and bans subsequent performances of his work in Ireland. This ban publicly announced in July but, as early as February, 1958, Beckett cancelled permission to Alan Simpson to stage *Endgame* at the Pike Theatre, Dublin. The ban on any production of his work in Ireland continued until 7th May, 1960.

October 28. *Endgame* and *Krapp's Last Tape* produced at the Royal Court Theatre, London. World première of *Krapp's Last Tape* in English.

1959   February 25. Beckett awarded D.Litt. (h.c.), Dublin University.

June 24. *Embers* first broadcast by B.B.C. London.

September 14. *Embers* awarded *Prix Italia* offered by Radio-televisione Italiana for literary and dramatic work on radio.

1960   January 25. *Act Without Words II* first performed at the Institute of Contemporary Arts, London.

1961   September 17. *Happy Days* produced at the Cherry Lane Theatre, New York. World première in English.

1962   October 5. *End of Day*, a late night entertainment from the works of Samuel Beckett, featuring solo performer Jack MacGowran, at the Gaiety Theatre, Dublin.

October 16. *End of Day* repeated at New Arts Theatre, London.

November 1. *Happy Days* produced at the Royal Court Theatre, London. British première.

November 13. *Words and Music* first broadcast by B.B.C. London.

1963 January 25. *Tous Ceux qui Tombent* first televised by O.R.T.F., Paris.

May 9. *Act Without Words I* presented on Telefís Éireann.

June 14. *Spiel,* (*Play*) first produced at Ulmer Theater, Ulm, Germany.

September 30. *Happy Days* produced at the Eblana Theatre, Dublin.

October 13. *Cascando* first broadcast in French by O.R.T.F., Paris.

October 21. *Oh, les Beaux Jours* (*Happy Days*) produced at the Odéon Theatre de France, Paris.

1964 January 4. *Play* produced at the Cherry Lane Theatre, New York. World première in English.

April 7. *Play* produced in English at the Old Vic, London. First British production.

June 14. *Comédie* (*Play*) produced at the Pavillon de Marsan, Paris.

July. Beckett working in New York on a film called *Project I* with Buster Keaton. The completed work was renamed *Film*.

October 6. *Cascando* first broadcast in English by B.B.C., London.

1965 February 23. *From Beginning to End,* a Beckett anthology, read by Jack MacGowran on B.B.C., London.

September 15. *Beginning to End,* a performance of work by Samuel Beckett, with Jack MacGowran, produced at the Lantern Theatre, Dublin.

October. *Film* awarded *Prix Filmcritice* at Venice Film Festival.

October 18. Has finished *Eh Joe,* a piece for television.

1966 January. *Film* awarded Special Jury Prize at International Film Festival of Short Subjects at Tours.

February 28. *Va et Viens (Come and Go)* produced at Odéon-Théâtre de France, Paris.

April 28. *Beginning to End* televised by Radio Telefis Eireann.

July 4. *Eh Joe* televised by B.B.C., London.

August. *Comédie,* the French film version of *Play,* shown at the Venice Biennale.

November. Jack MacGowran records, under Beckett's supervision, *MacGowran Speaking Beckett,* extracts from Beckett's work with musical interludes by J. Beckett, harmonium, E. Beckett, flute, and S. Beckett, gong, for Claddagh Records, Dublin.

1967 June. Beckett accepts invitation to have an experimental theatre at St. Peter's College, Oxford, named after him.

September 25. Beckett directs production of *Endgame* at Schiller-Theater, Berlin.

October 7. *Play* presented at the Abbey Theatre, Dublin.

November 9. *Happy Days* presented by Radio Telefis Eireann

1968 February 28. *Come and Go.* World première in English at the Peacock Theatre, Dublin.

1969 January 26. *All That Fall* presented by Radio Telefis Eireann.

1970 June 17. *Breath* given first American performance during the American première of *Oh! Calcutta!,* presented at the Eden Theatre, New York, after thirty-nine preview performances.

September. Beckett directs production of *Krapp's Last Tape* at the Schiller-Theater, Berlin.

October. First British presentation of *Breath* at the Close Theatre, Glasgow.

October 23. Beckett awarded Nobel Prize in Literature.

December 1. *Waiting for Godot* presented at the Abbey Theatre, Dublin.

December 7. *Cascando* (a recording of the B.B.C. production of October 6, 1964) presented by R.T.E.

1971 February. *Beginning to End*, Jack MacGowran's performance of works by Beckett presented in Paris.

March 8. Gala performance includes *Breath* at The Playhouse, Oxford, to launch campaign for Samuel Beckett Memorial Theatre.

September 9. *Krapp's Last Tape* presented by the Abbey Players at the Peacock Theatre, Dublin.

November. Presented as *Jack MacGowran in the Works of Samuel Beckett* at the Newman Theatre, New York.

February 26. First radio reading of Samuel Beckett's prose poem, *Lessness*, on B.B.C. Radio 3. The readers included Harold Pinter, Nicol Williamson, Donal Donnelly, Patrick Magee, Denys Hawthorne and Leonard Fenton.

The Plays

En Attendant Godot   *Waiting for Godot*

A tragi-comedy in Two Acts. (Title page, English edition)

"A play that is striving all the time to avoid definition." (Beckett.)
"A play in which nothing happens, *twice*." (V. Mercier.)
"I didn't choose to write a play — it just happened like that." (Beckett.)
"Je l'ai écrit d'une traite." (Beckett.)
"One act would have been too little and three acts would have been too much." (Beckett.)

Originally written in French between October, 1948, and January, 1949. Translated into English by the author by June, 1954.
Published in France, Editions de Minuit, Paris, December, 1952.
Published in America, Grove Press, New York, 1954.
Published in England, Faber and Faber, London, 1956. A revised text was published in 1965.

First production in France.
Théâtre de Babylone, Paris, January 5, 1953.
Directed by Roger Blin.
Cast: Vladimir — Lucien Raimbourg.
       Estragon — Pierre Latour.
       Pozzo — Roger Blin.
       Lucky — Jean Martin.
       Le petit garçon — Serge Lecointe.

First production in England.
Arts Theatre Club, London, August 3, 1955.
Directed by Peter Hall.
Cast: Vladimir — Paul Daneman.
       Estragon — Peter Woodthorpe.
       Pozzo — Peter Bull.
       Lucky — Timothy Bateson.
       A boy — Michael Walker.
This production transferred to the Criterion Theatre on September 12, 1955, and ran until May, 1956.

First production in Ireland.
The Pike Theatre, Dublin, October 28, 1955.
Directed by Alan Simpson.
Cast: Vladimir — Dermot Kelly
      Estragon — Austin Byrne.
      Pozzo — Nigel FitzGerald.
      Lucky — Donal Donnelly.
      A boy — Seamus Fitzmaurice.

First production in America.
The Coconut Grove Playhouse, Miami, January 3, 1956.
Directed by Alan Schneider.
Cast: Vladimir — Tom Ewell.
      Estragon — Bert Lahr.
      Pozzo — J. Scott Smart.
      Lucky — Arthur Malet.
      A boy — Jimmy Oster.

First production in New York.
John Golden Theatre, New York, April 19, 1956.
Directed by Herbert Berghorf.
Cast: Vladimir — E. G. Marshall.
      Estragon — Bert Lahr.
      Pozzo — Kurt Kusznar.
      Lucky — Alvin Epstein.
      A boy — Luchino Solito De Solis.

"It is gratifying to learn that the bulk of your audience was made up of young people. This was also the case in Paris, London, and throughout Germany. I must, after all, be less dead than I thought." (Beckett, quoted *New York Times*, September 21, 1958.)

SYNOPSIS

Scene: Act I. A country road. A tree. Evening.
       Act II. Next day. Same time. Same place.

Two men, Vladimir and Estragon, or Didi and Gogo as they call each other, are waiting on a deserted country road in an unspecified area for a Mr. Godot to come or for night to fall. They do not know Godot very well and they cannot be sure what they expect or even if they are waiting at the right place. No indication is given of how or

66

when this vigil began. Presently two other men appear, Pozzo, a tyrannical master, and Lucky, his abject and decrepit servant who has a rope tied round his neck for reins, and is driven with a whip. Pozzo eats his supper from a hamper which Lucky is carrying, and talks to Vladimir and Estragon. To amuse them, he makes Lucky dance and then "think", this latter performance being a long, incoherent tirade which the other three forcibly suppress. At length, master and servant move on towards a fair at which Pozzo says that he hopes to sell Lucky for a good price. Soon afterwards a boy arrives with a message from Mr. Godot. He will not come that night but will surely come the next. The boy goes. Vladimir and Estragon talk for a time, consider hanging themselves, decide to move on, but are still sitting motionless near the tree as the curtain falls. This situation, with slight variations, is repeated in Act II. The tree has sprouted four or five leaves overnight. Pozzo and Lucky re-appear, but now Pozzo is blind and Lucky is said to be dumb. Godot's messenger, although apparently the same boy as in Act I, insists that this is the first time that he has come. Be that as it may, the message itself remains the same. Again Vladimir and Estragon talk for a time, consider hanging themselves, decide to move on, but are still sitting motionless near the tree as the curtain falls.

All That Fall   *Tous Ceux Qui Tombent*

A Play for Radio. (Title page, English edition)

"It is a text written to come out of the dark." (Beckett.)

Originally written in English between June and November 11th, 1956, at the suggestion of a friend in the B.B.C. It is often stated that the work was commissioned but this phrase needs clarification. When the suggestion was put forward, Beckett promised nothing definite but said that he would try. He will not commit himself formally by signing a contract and accepting money in advance for something which he is not sure of being able to write.

Translated into French by Robert Pinget.

Published in England, Faber and Faber, London, 1957; in France, Editions de Minuit, Paris, 1957; in America, Grove Press, New York, 1957.

First broadcast in England.
B.B.C. Third Programme, London, January 13, 1957.
Directed by Donald McWhinnie.
Cast: Mrs. Rooney — Mary O'Farrell.
        Christy — Allan McClelland.
        Mr. Tyler — Brian O'Higgins.
        Mr. Slocum — Patrick Magee.
        Tommy — Jack MacGowran.
        Mr. Barrell — Harry Hutchinson.
        Miss Fitt — Sheila Ward.
        A Female Voice — Peggy Marshall.
        Mr. Rooney — J. G. Devlin.
        Jerry — Terrance Farrell.

First broadcast in France.
O.R.T.F., Paris, December 19, 1959.
Directed by Alain Trutat.
Cast: Mme. Rooney — Marise Paillet.
        Mons. Rooney — Roger Blin.

First televised in France.
O.R.T.F., Paris, February 25, 1963.
Directed by Michel Mitrani.
Cast: Mme. Rooney — Alice Sapricht.
      Mons. Rooney — Guy Tréjean.

First broadcast in Ireland.
R.T.E., Dublin, January 26, 1969.
Directed by Dan Treston.
Cast: Mrs. Rooney — Neasa Ní Annracháin.
      Christy — Dermot Crowley.
      Mr. Tyler — Eamonn Keane
      Mr. Slocum — Aidan Grennell.
      Tommy — Michael Campion.
      Mr. Barrell — Brian O'Higgins.
      Miss Fitt — Deirdre O'Meara
      A Female Voice — Patricia Moloney.
      Mr. Rooney — Thomas Studley.
      Jerry — Bosco Hogan.

SYNOPSIS

A fat, garrulous, old woman, Maddy Rooney, is making her way to Boghill, a country station, to meet her blind husband, Dan, returning from his office in the city. She passes a ruined house in which a woman is playing an old record of "Death and the Maiden". Then she is overtaken, first by Christy, a local carter who wants to sell her some dung, next by Mr. Tyler, a retired bill-server whom she sends away so that she may mourn her dead daughter, and finally by her old admirer, Mr. Slocum, clerk of the local racecourse, to which he is driving in his car. He offers her a lift and after great exertions by both of them, she is hoisted into the car and they set off for the station, killing a chicken on the way. When they arrive, there is the same trouble in getting Mrs. Rooney out of the vehicle but now Mr. Slocum is helped by Tommy, a porter. Mrs. Rooney is reluctantly assisted up the steps to the station by the sanctimonious Miss Fitt. A conversation ensues with the stationmaster, Mr. Barrell, who cannot explain why the train should be so late.

On its arrival, fifteen minutes behind time, Maddy at last finds her husband who greets her coolly, and they start off home. When she tries to find out what delayed the train, he is at first evasive, then gives a dramatized but quite uninformative account of the journey. This is interspersed with all kinds of talk about his possible retirement, the number of steps from the station to the road, a reminiscence from Maddy of a psychology lecture, Dan's misanthropic descriptions of domestic bliss, and his cheese-paring calculations. At one point Dan admits to a desire to murder a child, confessing that he had often considered attacking Jerry, the boy who usually leads him home from the station. Presently Jerry comes running after them with "an object like a ball" which Mr. Barrell says Dan has dropped. At first Dan denies this, then violently takes it and offers no explanation beyond the phrase "it is a thing which I carry about with me." Jerry starts back for the station but is recalled by Maddy who wants to know why the train was so late. Jerry tells her that a child had fallen from it under the wheels and had been killed. He then runs off and the Rooneys trudge on home through a tempest of wind and rain.

Fin de Partie   *Endgame*

A Play in One Act. (Title page, English edition)

"Rather difficult and elliptic, mostly depending on the power of the text to claw, more inhuman than *Godot*." (Beckett.)

"If *Godot* is the anguish of waiting, *Endgame* is the anguish of going." (Jack MacGowran.)

"In *Godot*, the audience wonders if Godot will ever come, in *Endgame*, it wonders if Clov will ever leave." (Attributed to Beckett.)

"La rédaction definitive de *Fin de Partie* est de '56. Mais j'avais abordé ce travail bien avant, peut-être en '54. Une première, puis une seconde version en deux actes ont précédé celle en un acte que vous connaissez." (Beckett.)

Originally written in French and dedicated to Roger Blin. Begun in 1954, completed in its present form by June 21, 1956. Translated into English by the author between April and August, 1957.

Published in France, Editions de Minuit, Paris, May, 1957.

Published in England, Faber and Faber, London, 1958.

Published in America, Grove Press, New York, 1958.

French version.
First production in England.
Royal Court Theatre, London, April 3, 1957.
Directed by Roger Blin.
Cast: Hamm — Roger Blin.
      Clov — Jean Martin.
      Nagg — Georges Adet.
      Nell — Christine Tsingos.

(Note. No French management would put on the play so its first production *in French* was in London. It was put on as a double bill with *Acte sans Paroles I*.)

First production in France.
Studio des Champs Elysées, Paris, April 26, 1957.
(It was put on as a double bill with *Acte Sans Paroles I*.)
Directed by Roger Blin.
Cast: Hamm — Roger Blin.
      Clov — Jean Martin.
      Nagg — Georges Adet.
      Nell — Germaine de France.

English version.
First production in America.
Cherry Lane Theatre, New York, January 28, 1958.
Directed by Alan Schneider.
Cast: Hamm — Lester Rawlins.
      Clov — Alvin Epstein.
      Nagg — P. J. Kelly.
      Nell — Nydia Westman.

First production in England.
Royal Court Theatre, London, October 28, 1958.
(It was put on as a double bill with *Krapp's Last Tape*.)
Directed by George Devine.
Cast: Hamm — George Devine.
      Clov — Jack MacGowran.
      Nagg — Richard Goolden.
      Nell — Frances Cuka.

First production in Ireland.
Dublin University Players Theatre, March 30, 1959.
(It was put on as a double bill with *Krapp's Last Tape*.)
Directed by Louis Lentin.
Cast: Hamm — Robert Somerset
      Clov — John Molloy.
      Nagg — David Nowlan.
      Nell — Sheila O'Sullivan.

SYNOPSIS

Scene: Bare interior. Grey light. Left and right back high up, two small windows. Front right a door. Hanging near door, its face to the window, a picture. Front left, touching each other are two ashbins. Centre, an armchair on castors. No indications are given of time or place but this "interior" is referred to as "the refuge". "Outside of here", says one character, Hamm, "it's death."

In the armchair sits Hamm, wearing dark glasses, a gold toque, a dressing-gown and thick socks. He is blind. He has a gaff with which he propels his chair like a punt, a whistle with which he summons Clov, and later on Clov brings him a toy dog with only three legs. In the ashbins are Nell and Nagg, his parents, both legless as the result of a cycling accident. The only character who can walk is Hamm's servant

72

Clov, but he cannot sit down. He is trying to leave Hamm, who persistently bullies him, making him push the chair round, open and shut the ashbins, carry and fetch, look through the windows with a telescope. Nell probably dies — but this is not explicitly stated. Hamm continues a story, "the one you have been telling yourself all your days", Clov kills a flea on his person and a rat in his kitchen, off stage. Looking through the window "for the last time" he sees what looks like a small boy. Clov retires to change into travelling clothes while Hamm discards his possessions one by one and settles back in his chair, covering his face with a blood-stained handkerchief. Clov appears at the door, with umbrella and bag, all ready for the road, but as the curtain falls he is still standing motionless on the threshold watching Hamm.

Acte Sans Paroles I   Act Without Words I

A Mime for One Player. (Title page, English edition.)

Originally written in French for the dancer, Deryk Mendel, in 1956 with music by John Beckett, the author's cousin. Translated into English by the author in 1958.

Published in France, Editions de Minuit, Paris, 1957.
Published in England, Faber and Faber, London, 1958.
Published in America, Grove Press, New York, 1958.

First production in England.
Royal Court Theatre, London, April 3, 1957.
(It was put on as a double bill with *Fin de Partie*.)
Danced and directed by Deryk Mendel.

First production in France.
Studio des Champs Elysées, Paris, April 27, 1957.
(It was put on as a double bill with *Fin de Partie*.)
Danced and directed by Deryk Mendel.

First production in Ireland.
Gaiety Theatre, Dublin, October 5, 1962 (as part of a Beckett programme, *End of Day*).
Danced by Jack MacGowran.
Directed by Donald MacWhinnie.
This production was filmed for transmission in a programme in the Spectrum series on Telefís Éireann.

SYNOPSIS

Scene: Desert, dazzling light. The man is flung backwards on stage from right wing. He falls, gets up immediately, dusts himself, turns aside and reflects. There is a whistle from the right wing and the man attempts to go out right. He is immediately flung backwards onto the stage. He falls, gets up, dusts himself, reflects. There is a whistle from the left wing. He tries to go out left. He is immediately flung backwards on to the stage. He falls, gets up, dusts himself, turns aside, reflects. There is another whistle from the left wing. He starts to go towards it, then thinks better of it, halts, turns aside and reflects. From now on he is subjected to a series of frustrations involving a palm tree, which might, but never will, give him shade, scissors and a rope with

74

which he might, but never can, hang himself, a carafe of water, which he might, but never can, reach and two cubes which might have helped him in all these things. Whenever he tries to achieve anything, including suicide, he is defeated; even when he uses his intelligence, he fails. He is summoned or goaded to each attempt by the whistle, but at last he ignores even that and, as the curtain falls, he lies on his side on the empty stage, looking at his hands.

Krapp's Last Tape   *La Dernière Bande*

Originally written in English for the actor, Patrick Magee. Completed by May, 1958. Translated into French in 1958 or 1959 by Pierre Leyris with the collaboration of the author.

Published in America, *Evergreen Review*, II, No. 5, New York, Summer, 1958.

Published in England, Faber and Faber, London, 1959.

Published in France, *Lettres Nouvelles*, Paris, March 4, 1959.

First production in England.
Royal Court Theatre, London, October 28, 1958.
(It was put on as a double bill with *Endgame*.)
Directed by Donald McWhinnie.
Cast: Krapp — Patrick Magee.

First production in France.
Théâtre Récamier, Paris, March 22, 1960.
Directed by Roger Blin.
Cast: Krapp — R. J. Chauffard.

First production in Ireland.
Dublin University Players Theatre, Dublin, March 30, 1959.
(It was put on as a double bill with *Endgame*.)
Directed by Louis Lentin.
Cast: Krapp — David Kelly.

Second Irish production.
Queen's Theatre, Dublin, June 20, 1960.
(It was put on as a double bill with Shaw's *Arms and the Man*.)
Directed by Godfrey Quigley.
Cast: Krapp — Cyril Cusack.

The score for an opera, *Krapp, ou la Dernière Bande* was composed by Marcel Mihalovici, working in close collaboration with Beckett. This was performed 'en concert' at the Théâtre Nationale Populaire on February 13, 1961, the orchestra being conducted by Serge Baudo. A German version with libretto by Elmar Tophoven was sung by William Dooley at the Théâtre des Nations on July 3, 1961, and a French version was broadcast by O.R.T.F. on May 16, 1961, with

Deryk Olsen as Krapp. Beckett himself has prepared an English version.

SYNOPSIS

Scene: A late evening in the future. Krapp's den.

All that can be seen are a table and chair standing in a pool of strong light; the rest is in darkness. On the table are a tape-recorder, a microphone, and some boxes containing spools of tape. At the table sits Krapp, an old man dingily dressed — "with a surprising pair of dirty, white boots, size ten at least, very pointed and narrow," White-faced with a purple nose, Krapp is grey-haired, dishevelled, near-sighted, hard of hearing, and has a cracked voice which has, however, kept its distinctive intonation. He walks laboriously.

Krapp begins by eating two bananas kept in a locked drawer of the table, then shambles off into the darkness where he noisily uncorks a bottle and drinks. He returns, consults a ledger and finds a tape "box 3, spool 5", lingering with great satisfaction over the word "spool". According to the ledger entry, this tape contains sections indexed as "Mother at rest at last, The black ball, The dark nurse, Slight improvement in bowel condition, Memorable equinox, and Farewell to love". Krapp puts on this tape made on his thirty-ninth birthday; the voice is strong, pompous yet unmistakably his at a much earlier time. At one point he goes off stage and returns with a dictionary in which he looks up "viduity", a word he had used on the tape. He omits certain passages, replays others, and finally, after another drink off stage, this time involving a syphon, he brings himself to start making the tape, his sixty-ninth birthday. He begins briskly enough, but soon tires of his task and sinks back into memories of the past. Presently he abandons the attempt altogether, replaces the earlier tape, plays over the final section again, and, as the curtain falls, he is sitting motionless, staring before him, while the tape runs on in silence.

In fact three tapes are involved in the play.

Tape I. We never hear this but Krapp-at-39 describes it on tape II which we do hear. According to Krapp-at-39, tape I was made "ten or twelve years ago", presumably on his twenty-seventh, twenty-eighth or twenty-ninth birthday. It mentions an unhappy love affair now over, with a girl called Bianca, "not much about her," Krapp-at-39 reports, "apart from a tribute to her eyes" and there are references to certain "aspirations" and resolutions — "to drink less and lead a less engrossing sexual life". This tape also contains a description of his father's last illness, of his own "flagging pursuit of happiness" and there is talk about his constipation and the *magnum opus* yet to come. The tape ends with what Krapp-at-39 describes as "a yelp to Providence."

Tape II. This, played on stage by Krapp-at-69, was made thirty years before when he was "sound as a bell, apart from my old weakness", presumably the constipation, and when "intellectually", he had every reason to suspect himself "at the . . . . (*hesitates*) . . . . crest of the wave — or thereabouts". On this tape we hear an account of how Krapp waited for his mother's death, of a love scene in a punt, the termination of another love affair, and of the moment when Krapp-at-39 "saw the whole thing", "the vision at last," but Krapp-at-69 angrily turns this off. The tape ends, "Perhaps my best years are gone. When there was a chance of happiness. But I wouldn't want them back. Not with the fire in me now. No, I wouldn't want them back."

Tape III. This, which Krapp-at-69 now attempts to make, begins with a sneer at the voice on tape II, just as tape II had begun with a sneer at the voice on tape I, but Krapp-at-69 admits that tape II had "Everything there, everything on this old muckball, all the light and dark and famine and feasting of . . . . . (*hesitates*) . . . . . the ages!" Of the past year, Krapp-at-69 has little to report. The *magnum opus* has sold seventeen copies, "of which eleven at trade price to free circulating libraries beyond the seas." He recalls sessions with Fanny, "Bony old ghost of a whore", and a visit to Vespers when he went to sleep and fell off the pew. Here he tires of "this drivel" and imagines himself propped up in bed, in the dark, wandering through the past. "Be again, be again", he says, "all that old misery. Once wasn't enough for you". He quotes from the love scene on tape II, and wrenching off tape III, throws it away.

Acte Sans Paroles II   *Act Without Words II*

A Mime for two players. (Title page, English edition)

Originally written in French, probably early 1958, and translated by the author into English. It may have been one of the "mimes of my devising" offered by Beckett to the 1958 Dublin Theatre Festival but withdrawn by him in February of that year following the decision of the Festival Committee to drop O'Casey's play, *The Drums of Father Ned*.

Published in England, *New Departures I*, London, Summer, 1959.
Published in America, Grove Press, New York, 1960.
Published in France, Editions de Minuit, Paris, 1966.

First production in England.
Institute of Contemporary Arts, London, January 25, 1960.
Directed by Michael Horovitz.
Cast: A — David Webster.
       B — Donal Donnelly.

SYNOPSIS.

This mime is to be played "on a low platform at the back of the stage, violently lit in its entire length; the rest of the stage being in darkness. Frieze effect".

At the beginning of the piece there are two sacks at the right of the stage with a man in each, and a neatly folded pile of clothes between them. A goad with no wheels comes on stage from right and pierces the nearer sack which contains A. He does not move. The goad recoils, strikes again and A now moves, whereupon it withdraws. A, "slow, awkward — absent" crawls out of his sack, clad in a shirt and, brooding between every action, prays, takes a pill, puts on the clothes, bites but spits out a piece of partly eaten carrot, and with great effort carries both sacks towards the centre of the stage. He puts them down, his own nearer to the left, then, still brooding between each action, he takes off the clothes, except his shirt, drops them untidily on to the stage, takes a pill, kneels, prays, and crawls back into his sack.

The goad now appears, still from the right, but on one wheel, and pierces the sack nearest to it, namely that occupied by B. In contrast to A, B is "brisk, rapid, and precise" so that although he gets through a great deal more than A, their periods of action outside the sacks are about the same.

79

B needs only one touch of the goad and never broods or prays. He frequently consults a large watch, however, as clad in his shirt he does his exercises, brushes his teeth, rubs his scalp, combs his hair, puts on the clothes, brushes them and his hair, inspects himself in a mirror, eats a carrot with obvious enjoyment, and refers to a map and compasses. He then picks up the two sacks and carries them even further left where he puts them down. A is now nearer to the right of the stage. Still constantly referring to the watch, B again performs his toilet and his exercises, remembers to re-wind the watch, undresses, piles the clothes neatly between the sacks, and crawls into his own.

The goad, now on two wheels but still entering from the right, pierces A's sack once without effect. It strikes a second time, A moves, and the goad withdraws.

A Play in Two Acts. (Title page, English edition.)

Originally written in English in 1961, and translated into French by the author.

Published in America, Grove Press, New York, 1961.

Published in England, Faber and Faber, London, 1963.

Published in France, Editions de Minuit, Paris, 1963.

First production in America.

Cherry Lane Theatre, New York, September 17, 1961.

Directed by Alan Schneider.

Cast: Winnie — Ruth White.
      Willie — John C. Becher.

First production in England.

Royal Court Theatre, London, November 1, 1962.

Directed by George Devine.

Cast: Winnie — Brenda Bruce.
      Willie — Peter Duguid.

First production in France.

Odéon-Théâtre de France, Paris, October 21, 1963.

Directed by Roger Blin.

Cast: Winnie — Madeleine Renaud.
      Willie — Jean-Louis Barrault.

First production in Ireland.

Eblana Theatre, Dublin, September 30, 1963.

Directed by John Berry.

Cast: Winnie — Marie Kean.
      Willie — O. Z. Whitehead.

A television production, with the same cast, directed by Chloe Gibson, was transmitted by Radio Telefís Éireann on November 9, 1967.

SYNOPSIS

Scene: Expanse of scorched grass, rising centre to low mound. Gentle slopes at side but sharper drop at back.

In Act I, buried to her waist in the exact centre of the mound stands Winnie, a woman of about fifty, well-preserved, blonde for preference. She can move her arms and handle her few possessions, a toothbrush, a tube of toothpaste, a parasol, a small mirror, a revolver, a handkerchief, and spectacles. At the back of the mound lives her husband, Willie, a man of about sixty who can only move on all fours and who passes his day reading a newspaper or looking at a naughty postcard. Winnie's waking and sleeping are governed by a bell offstage. She spends her time talking, reminiscing, looking at Willie, and taking care of her appearance. Occasionally she breaks down but always manages to pull herself together and put a brave face on things.

In Act II she is embedded to the neck and cannot even move her head. Her possessions are still there, but are useful only as a subject for talk. She now invents stories to help while away the hours between the bell for waking and the bell for sleeping. Willie has been silent for a long time, but suddenly he appears in front of the mound, "dressed to kill", and makes a great effort to crawl up to Winnie, who can no longer give him a hand as she might have done previously. Willie falls back twice but Winnie finds in his visit plenty to make this "one more happy day". She sings the waltz from *The Merry Widow,* looking straight at Willie, who is staring at her from the foot of the mound as the curtain falls.

A Play in One Act. (Title page, English edition.)

Originally written in English, probably in 1963. Translated into French by the author, and into German by Elmar Tophoven.
Published in England, Faber and Faber, London, 1964.
Published in France, Editions de Minuit, Paris, 1966.

First production in Germany.
Ulmer Theater, Ulm-Donau, Germany, June 14, 1963.
Directed by Deryk Mendel.
Cast: f.1 First Woman — Nancy Illig.
        f.2 Second Woman — Sigrid Pfeiffer.
        m. Man — Gerhard Winter.

First production in America.
Cherry Lane Theatre, New York, January 4, 1964.
Directed by Alan Schneider.
Cast: First Woman — Frances Sternhagen.
        Second Woman — Marian Reardon.
        Man — Michael Lipton.

First production in England.
Old Vic Theatre, London, April 7, 1964.
Directed by George Devine.
Cast: w.1 First Woman — Rosemary Harris.
        w.2 Second Woman — Billie Whitelaw.
        m. Man — Robert Stephens.

First production in France.
Pavillon de Marsan, Paris, June 14, 1964.
Directed by Jean-Marie Serreau.
Cast: f.1 First Woman — Eléonore Hirt.
        f.2 Second Woman — Delphine Seyrig.
        h. Man — Michael Lonsdale.

First production in Ireland.
Abbey Theatre, Dublin, October 7, 1967.
Directed by Edward Golden.
Cast: w.1 — Joan O'Hara.
        m. — Patrick Laffan.
        w.2 — Angela Newman.

SYNOPSIS

The curtain rises on a dark stage on which stand three urns containing w1, m and w2. For a more detailed description see *supra* page 35 *et seq.*

Embers

Words and Music

Cascando

INTRODUCTORY NOTE

These three works, 'a play written specially for broadcasting' and 'two short pieces for radio', are conceived in terms of sound without sight. No certain line divides the exterior world from that within the skulls of the characters. In *Embers*, for example, we hear the voice of a woman, Ada — Henry's wife. We are not told, however, whether she is actually present sitting beside Henry, or whether she is an abstraction in his mind like his dead father whom he also imagines sitting beside him, but whose voice is never heard. Ambiguity, abstraction, these are the possibilities peculiar to sound radio which Beckett is exploiting here to the full. Thus we have impact, not argument. It would, therefore, be pointless and indeed wrong-headed to attempt any formal synopses of the 'stories'. Such synopses could only be personal visualizations of sounds and no more valid than a personal visualization of, say, the Pastoral Symphony. Instead, and largely for purposes of identification, a description of each piece is offered.

Embers   *Cendres*

A New Play written specially for Broadcasting
(Title page, English edition)

Originally written in English and completed by 1959. Awarded *Prix Italia* by Radiotelevisione Italiana, 1959. Translated into French by the author and Robert Pinget.
Published in England, Faber and Faber, London, 1959.
Published in France, Editions de Minuit, Paris, 1959.
Published in America, Grove Press, New York, 1960.

First broadcast in England.
B.B.C. Third Programme, June 24, 1959.
Directed by Donald McWhinnie.
Cast: Henry — Jack MacGowran.
       Ada — Kathleen Michael.
       Addie — Kathleen Helme.
       Music master/Riding master — Patrick Magee.

DESCRIPTION

The principal speaker in the play is called Henry. He is heard walking near the sea and later sitting down for a time. He recalls his dead father whom we do not hear. He also calls for "Hooves!" and we hear the sound of hooves walking on a hard road. They die rapidly away but are once more audible when Henry calls for them. In the same way we hear the sound of Henry's wife, Ada, and of a music lesson and of a riding lesson given to his daughter, Addie, both of which end in Addie weeping hysterically. Henry tells himself a story involving two characters, Bolton and Holloway, which contains a notable passage describing a silent confrontation between the two old men in Bolton's house late at night.

Words and Music   *Paroles et Musique*

A Short Piece for Radio (Title page, English edition.)

Originally written in English in 1962, and translated into French by the author.

Published in America, *Evergreen Review,* See p. 76, New York, VI, No. 27, November-December, 1962.

Published in England, Faber & Faber, London, 1964.

Published in France, Editions de Minuit, Paris, 1966.

First broadcast in England.

B.B.C. Third Programme, November 13, 1962.

Directed by Michael Bakewell.

Cast: Croak — Felix Felton.

Words — Patrick Magee.

DESCRIPTION

Croak has two servants, Words, whom he calls Joe, and Music, whom he calls Bob. One evening while waiting to perform for him, Words (or Joe) rehearses a piece of prose on "sloth" — a turgid mass of platitude which disintegrates in the same way as Lucky's tirade in *Waiting for Godot*. When Croak arrives, he apologises for being late, speaks of a face seen on the stair, and declares the theme for the evening to be "love". Words recites the tirade he has been rehearsing, substituting "love" for "sloth" but not always even remembering to do that. From time to time, Croak, by banging a club on the floor, stops Words and invokes Music who replies with suitable themes. There is no *consensus* between Words and Music but gradually two lyrics are built up and sung, rather badly, by Words. Finally Croak can stand no more of it and shuffles off, leaving the other two still unreconciled.

Cascando

A Radio Piece for Music and Voice. (Title page, English edition.)

The play is "about the character called Woburn who never appears." (Beckett.)

Originally written in French, at the request of the composer of the music, Marcel Mihalovici. Translated into English by the author.
Published in France, Editions de Minuit, Paris, 1963.
Published in America, *Evergreen Review*, See p. 74, New York, VII, No. 30, May-June, 1963.
Published in England, Faber & Faber, London, 1964.

First broadcast in France.
O.R.T.F., Paris, October 13, 1963.
Directed by Roger Blin.
Cast: L'Ouvreur — Roger Blin.
La Voix — Jean Martin.

First broadcast in England.
B.B.C. Third Programme, October 6, 1964.
Directed by Donald McWhinnie.
Cast: Opener — Denys Hawthorne.
Voice — Patrick Magee.

DESCRIPTION

Like *Words and Music,* this is essentially an experience in sound and tempo, not sight and sequence. Instead of Croak, we have an Opener; instead of Words, there is Voice "low, panting", striving to tell a story. If he can tell the right story, then Voice will be allowed to be forever silent. The Opener can bring in the Voice and the Music separately or together. The Opener denies that the sounds are, as some say, in his head. "It's my life", he says, "I live on that". And he adds "There is nothing in my head".

Sometimes Voice describes the movements and actions of a man called Woburn. Sometimes he seems to be encouraging himself. The play ends with one of these passages very similar to two earlier ones:

VOICE : *(together)* MUSIC :	— this time . . . . it's the right one . . . . finish . . . . no more stories . . . sleep . . we're there . . . . nearly . . . . just a few more . . . . don't let . . . . go . . . Woburn . . . he cling on . . . . come on . . . . Come on . . . .

. . . .

Silence.

CURTAIN.

Film

"Esse est percipi.

All extraneous perception suppressed, animal, human, divine, self-perception maintains in being.

Search on non-being in flight from extraneous perception breaking down in inescapability of self-perception.

No truth value attaches to above, regarded as of merely structural and dramatic convenience". (Beckett.)

The project for *Film* was originally written in English about 1964 at the suggestion of Barney Rosset of the Grove Press, New York. The film was produced by Evergreen Films and shot in New York in the summer of that year. Awarded the *Prix Filmcritice* at the Venice Film Festival in October, 1965, and a Special Jury Prize at the International Film Festival of Short Subjects at Tours in January, 1966.

Published in England, Faber and Faber, London, 1967.
Published in America, Grove Press, New York, 1969.

Directed by Alan Schneider.
Cast: The Man — Buster Keaton.
      The Couple — James Karen
                Susan Reed.
      The Flower-seller — Nell Harrison.

SYNOPSIS

The film begins with a human eye opening very slowly. Then with the camera (or Eye$=$E) we pursue a man (the Object$=$O). Beckett establishes a convention whereby as long as the angle between E and O is less than $45°$ the victim does not know that he is being seen. Once the angle is widened, however, the Object feels and visibly registers the anguish of perceivedness. To illustrate this we are shown the effects of this anguish upon an elderly couple and on a flower-seller, all three accidental objects of perception. The Eye's concern is with the Object whom it follows along a street, into a house and finally into a room. Here the man draws the curtains, puts out the dog and cat, tears down from the wall a picture of a god with protruding eyes, covers a cage containing a watchful parrot, and a bowl in which swims a staring goldfish. Settling himself in a rocking-chair he looks through a wallet of photographs of himself from infancy to middle age. He tears these up one by one and then rocks himself into a sleep or oblivion from which the camera inadvertently awakens him, but he soon drops off again. After a much more cautious approach, the camera ends up directly in front of its victim. The man wakes up, is brought face to face with his tireless pursuer — now seen to be himself—and when confronted with this self-perception, he sinks back into the chair, his head bowed between his hands.

Eh Joe   Dis Joe

A Piece for Television (Title page, English edition.)

Originally written in English for Jack MacGowran and finished by October 18, 1965. Translated into French by the author.
Published in England, Faber and Faber, London, 1967.
Published in France, Éditions de Minuit, Paris, 1966.

Televised by B.B.C., London, July 4, 1956.
Produced by Michael Bakewell.
Cast: Joe—Jack MacGowran.
The Voice—Sian Phillips.

DESCRIPTION

We *see* Joe, a man in his late fifties, in an old dressing-gown and carpet slippers in his room. Having opened and closed the window, drawn the curtains, locked the door and cupboard, looked under the bed, Joe relaxes. When the Voice begins, Joe becomes intent. Thereafter, his face remains impassive except when it reflects the mounting tension of listening or on occasions when it shows varying degrees of relaxation as the Voice pauses, and Joe thinks that perhaps it has "relented for the evening".

We *hear* the Voice, a woman's, distant, remote, almost colourless, speaking in an absolutely steady rhythm and slightly more slowly than normal. It reminds Joe of the other voices he has heard in his head and his method of strangling them, "mental thuggee", as he calls the process, and it goes on to describe in great detail the suicide of a girl, not the speaker, whom Joe had loved and rejected. The story is punctuated by pauses during which the camera moves in upon Joe until finally it achieves "maximum close-up of his face", then voice and image are both extinguished.

92

Come and Go   *Va et Viens*

A Dramaticule. (Title page, English edition.)

"Beckett has very nearly made a play out of silences". (Hugh Kenner.)

Originally written in English at the beginning of 1966 and dedicated to John Calder. Translated into French by the author and into German by Elmar Tophoven.
Published in England, Calder and Boyars, London, 1967.
Published in France, Editions de Minuit, Paris, 1966.

First production in Germany.
Schiller Theater, Berlin, September, 1965.
Directed by Deryk Mendel.
Cast: Flo — Lieselotte Rau.
       Vi — Charlotte Foeres.
       Ru — Sibylle Gilles.

First production in France.
Odéon-Théâtre de France, Paris, February 28, 1966.
Directed by Jean-Marie Serreau.
Cast: Flo — Annie Bertin.
       Vi — Madeleine Renaud.
       Ru — Simone Valère.

First production in Ireland.
The Abbey Theatre Company at the Peacock Theatre, Dublin, February 28, 1968.
World premiêre in English.
Directed by Edward Golden.
Cast: Flo — Deirdre Purcell.
       Vi — Maire O'Neill.
       Ru — Kathleen Barrington.

First production in England.
Royal Festival Hall, London, December 9, 1968.
Directed by Deryk Mendel.
Cast: Flo — Marie Keane.
       Vi — Billie Whitelaw.
       Ru — Adrienne Corri.

DESCRIPTION

Three women, Flo, Vi and Ru of 'undeterminable' age are sitting on a bench in a pool of soft white light in the middle of a dark stage. They wear full-length coats of different colours and hats with brims wide enough to shade their faces. Apart from the different coloured coats, the three figures should be as alike as possible. After a silence, one sentence from Vi and a reply from Ru, Vi who has been sitting in the centre gets up and walks off into the darkness. Flo moves along to the centre of the bench next to Ru, to whom she confides some terrible secret about Vi, perhaps concerning her health. Vi, who, Flo hopes, does not know the truth, returns and now sits in the space vacated by Flo. Two more sentences of reminiscence follow. Flo rises and walks off into the darkness. Ru then moves along to the centre of the bench next to Vi, to whom she confides some terrible secret, possibly about Flo's health. Flo returns and sits in the place vacated by Ru. Two more sentences of reminiscence, then Ru rises and walks off into the darkness. Vi moves to the centre of the bench next to Flo to whom she confides some terrible secret, maybe about Ru's health. Ru returns and sits in the place vacated by Vi. Then they hold hands 'in the old way' as they did at school and as people do when singing " Auld Lang Syne". i.e. Ru holds one of Vi's hands and one of Flo's, Vi holds one of Ru's and one of Flo's, Flo holds one of Ru's and one of Vi's. Flo says that she can feel the rings. We can see that there are no rings. The three sit in silence as the curtain falls.

In the play there are 121 words, 23 speeches, 12 silences, and the piece runs for three minutes.

Breath

Originally written in English in response to an invitation by Kenneth Tynan.

Published in England in *Gambit*, No. 16, Calder and Boyars, London, 1970.

Published in America in *Oh! Calcutta!*, Grove Press, New York; (paperback), 1969.

Corrected text published in America in *Oh! Calcutta!*, Grove Press, New York, (hardback), 1969.

First production in America.
Eden Theatre, New York City, June 17, 1969.
Presented as the prologue to *Oh! Calcutta!*, which, under the direction of Jacques Levy, opened after 39 preview performances.

First production in Britain.
Close Theatre, Glasgow, October, 1969.
Directed by Geoffrey Gilham.

TEXT*

CURTAIN

1. Faint light on stage littered with miscellaneous rubbish. Hold about five seconds.

2. Faint brief cry and immediately inspiration and slow increase of light together reaching maximum together in about ten seconds. Silence and hold about five seconds.

3. Expiration and slow decrease of light together reaching minimum together (light as in 1) in about ten seconds and immediately cry as before. Silence and hold about five seconds.

CURTAIN

RUBBISH No verticals, all scattered and lying.

CRY Instant of recorded vagitus. Important that two cries be identical, switching on and off strictly synchronised light and breath.

BREATH Amplified recording.

MAXIMUM LIGHT Not bright. If 0 = dark and 10 = bright, light should move from about 3 to 6 and back.

—*Samuel Beckett*

338 2 2195